Dark Days

*Reminiscences of the War in Hong Kong and
Life in China, 1941–1945*

TAN KHENG YEANG

Order this book online at www.trafford.com
or email orders@trafford.com

Most Trafford titles are also available at major online book retailers.

Printed in the United States of America.

ISBN: 978-1-4269-5089-6 (sc)
ISBN: 978-1-4269-5090-2 (hc)
ISBN: 978-1-4269-5091-9 (e)

Library of Congress Control Number: 2011900350

Trafford rev. 03/30/2011

 www.trafford.com

North America & international
toll-free: 1 888 232 4444 (USA & Canada)
phone: 250 383 6864 ✦ fax: 812 355 4082

Other books by the same author

Fiction

Novels
Conflict in the Home
Sauce of Life
Struggle Toward Extinction
Motivating Forces

Poetry
Diverse Modes
Poems (Flowery Country/Sun and Rain/Grains of Sand)

Non-Fiction

Philosophy
Intrinsic to Universe
The Material Structure

Sayings
Reduced Reflections

Linguistics
LUIF: A New Language
LUIF Dictionaries

Acknowledgement

"The author wishes to thank Ms. Valerie Cameron
for her invaluable assistance in preparing the manuscript of
this book for publication."

In memory of my parents

This book of reminiscences deals initially with the fall of Hong Kong in 1941. The scene then shifts to South China in the war years from 1942 to 1945. It portrays the lives of ordinary people in the dark days brought on by rampart militarism.

Contents

1. Before the Pacific War   1

2. Those Eighteen Fateful Days   8

3. Under Japanese Rule   16

4. Exclusive Exploitation Sphere   24

5. The Ugly Face of Conquest   30

6. Discourses and Conversations   37

7. Later Events   44

8. Departure   51

9. Kukong   58

10. In a Train   65

11. The Sino-Japanese War   71

12. Life in Kweilin   78

13. Liuchow   85

14. Crisis   92

15. An Inland Journey   98

16. Loping   104

17. Kunming   112

18. War's End   118

19. Return Journey   125

20. Hong Kong Again   132

Southern China

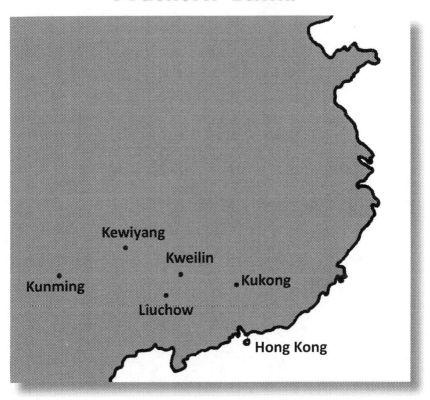

1. Before the Pacific War

Before the great port of Hong Kong fell into the hands of the Japanese aggressors in 1941, it had never formed the scene of any warfare from the day it started off its career as a British colony in 1841. In a matter of weeks, a splendid city became a region of misery and glad were its inhabitants to shake its dust from their feet and disperse themselves over the cities and villages in Free China. I lived there for years as a student of civil engineering at Hong Kong University; I saw the battle for the island, and for months afterward I witnessed and endured its terrors.

Hong Kong is situated just south of the Tropic of Cancer and is therefore a subtropical region. Its land, having a total area of nearly four hundred square miles, comprises the island of Hong Kong, which is only twenty-nine square miles in extent, a number of other islands in the vicinity, Kowloon on the mainland opposite, and the New Territories. It is the island, or rather the city, of Victoria located on its northern side that constitutes the important section of the colony. Hills on the island rise sheer from the shore toward its center. Kowloon is flat land, but it is ringed by mountains that extend to its hinterland of the New Territories.

How peaceful life was before the Pacific War! The daily round, the common task, possessed a charm that perhaps was not adequately appreciated, as men seldom realize keenly the value of what is taken for granted in the same way that presumably birds do not regard their gift of flight as wonderful. It was good to breathe then. It was pleasant to watch the teeming streets, the red buses swallowing and disgorging passengers as they paused uneasily, impatient to hurry on, the glitter of neon lights, the vessels of all nations in one of the finest harbors in the world, the panorama of tiers upon tiers of laughing lights before the spectator as he sat in a ferry

1

launch crossing over from Kowloon to Victoria. There was an abundance of the necessities and conveniences requisite for the maintenance of a vast population, and prices—though they rose slightly under the shadow of war in other arenas—were reasonable.

Hong Kong possesses a pleasant climate; summer alternates with winter, but the former is not too hot nor is the latter too cold. Its scenery is glamorous. What view could be more enchanting than the rippling waters of Repulse Bay? What sunset could rival that as viewed from the Peak, the large, crimson sun low on the horizon, elfish enough to set in vibration the lyrical strings of even the hardest heart? What could be more exhilarating than a ramble through the New Territories with its pines and coves?

The only natural phenomenon that is grievous is the typhoon, which tears through the place and is liable to wreak extensive damage; ships in the harbor can be thrown on the rocks, and houses in the city have their roofs driven in and windows wrenched off. But natural calamities are never as disastrous as those engendered by man. There were then no scowling sentries holding grim bayonets to molest passersby and to deform the smiling face of the fair countryside. Barbed-wire barricades, in all their ugliness, and multitudinous prohibited areas were unknown. Everyone was free to roam where he pleased and gaze at any beautiful scene that took his fancy.

Numerous people flocked to the beaches in summer to enjoy a dip in the sea, for the place was bespangled with swimming resorts. Bathing pavilions were much in evidence. The populace took to swimming as their chief recreation. Even when dragon boat races were being held on the fifth day of the fifth moon to commemorate the death of a great historical hero, Ch'ǔ Yǔan, there was sure to be a crowd of boys and girls floating around near the piers, where the boats arrived to the clamorous accompaniment of drums, not guns. Launch picnics to the neighboring islands were popular. Nothing could equal the happiness of the participants as they stood, basket in hand, waiting for the arrival of the boats. One could also go for long rambles among the hills and trace the courses of the enticing streams.

The people of Hong Kong were nearly all Chinese, the preponderant majority being Cantonese. For the greater part, they or their forefathers came from the neighboring province of Kwangtung, to which the colony originally belonged. Their way of life and their ideas were basically Chinese and only superficially Western. They could go to Canton and easily slide into its society; they wouldn't find that they would be a square peg in a round hole in respect to anything. There was free movement between

China and Hong Kong, and there were those who traversed the border regularly. Cultural compartmentalization was not likely to develop.

Hong Kong was primarily a commercial metropolis, and the people's lives centered on the earning of a livelihood and the acquisition of wealth. There was nothing to stir their interest in other directions. They left politics alone, being apparently quite content with their exclusion from all say in affairs of state. They experienced no yearning for cultural activities, and they produced no philosophers, scientists, or literary figures. They were pacific and would not know how to fight, for they had not received any military training.

Capitalism, pure and simple, constituted the basis of the economy. A few became rich, and there was a small class of professional men and a bigger class of small businessmen, but the majority were laborers who barely scratched a living. This urban proletariat was, however, not given to struggling for the realization of a communist society. It felt no urge to unite with the workers of the world.

Hong Kong was a free port devoted to the promotion of commerce, the import and export trade being its lifeblood. Its emporiums and shops sold goods from any part of the world, from Europe and America as well as China and other parts of Asia. Prices were cheap compared to those prevailing elsewhere. Swiss watches, Kodak cameras, carved camphorwood chests, radio sets, leatherware, carpets, embroidered fabrics, electrical appliances, silks and woolens, blackwood furniture, ceramics, antiques, ivory curios, jade carvings, jewelry—whatever merchandise was wanted by any person, resident or tourist, it was available.

The life in the streets was intense. Two-decker trams rattled along Des Voeux Road, red buses traveled everywhere, and taxis and cars claimed the same narrow streets as rickshaws and bicycles. Pedestrians jostled on the pavements, and crowds walked up and down the stepped streets. As one strolled along, one could see gray-headed fortune-tellers in skullcaps and long gowns revealing the mysteries of the future to anxious clients, craftsmen carving ivory balls with painstaking industry, calligraphists inditing scrolls, and shoe-shine boys happily plying their trade and running after potential clients. Open-air markets existed in certain streets, the stalls piled with vegetables, fruits, sausages, eggs, and a whole host of other comestibles, and customers moved around, among them girls carrying babies in crimson slings on their backs.

As the roads of Victoria were hacked out of the hillside, they were rarely straight or level. In the heart of the city, main streets could be

3

joined by steep lanes constructed as flights of steps, these "ladder streets" the preserve of pedestrians. Until I became more accustomed to it, I felt it odd to stand on one road and look down on the roofs of the houses below. The jumble of streets presented a picturesque scene.

The buildings were a mixed lot of Eastern and Western styles of architecture, a phenomenon quite common in the cities of the Orient of the twentieth century. Multistoried apartment stores reared their concrete structures in all their straight starkness, and banks of gray granite built in the Victorian Age displayed their dreary respectability. Rows of brick shophouses flourished in all their congestion. Fine, spacious villas set in blossomy gardens were visible. So too were tenement houses of a few stories, containing cubicles choked with sweltering humanity. They had verandas from which protruded poles hung with washing, fluttering like flags in the breeze. Then there were the stalls in the streets in all their disarray, constructed of all sorts of flimsy materials, from timber to canvas.

To see the sights one could pay a visit to Victoria Peak, otherwise known simply as the Peak, which towered above the Central District to a height of more than 1,800 feet. This place was used not merely for recreation with a few houses perched here and there (as with so many hills in other parts of the world), but as a residential area containing the best mansions in the colony. Ascent up the steep hillside was in trams hauled up by steel cables. From the terminus, about 1,300 feet high, a splendid view of the city, the harbor, Kowloon, and the mountains of the hinterland in the distance saluted the enraptured spectator. One could go to Repulse Bay engirdled by green hills, the blue water lapping a glorious beach of fine white sand. There were other good beach resorts, such as Deep Water Bay, South Bay, Stanley, Shek O, and Big Wave Bay, but this was the most popular. Then there was Aberdeen, a fishing village for more than a century, situated on the southwest corner of the island, with a great assemblage of thousands of boats rocking in its narrow harbor, the homes of families for generation after generation.

The harbor, with its area of twenty-three square miles surrounded almost entirely by land, was justly celebrated. It was as picturesque as it was busy. Vessels sailed into it from the east through the Lyemun Pass, the name of a narrow strait between Shaukiwan in Hong Kong and the New Territories. The harbor was never free of ocean liners, freighters, launches, junks, and sampans in all their seeming disarray. It was a splendid sight by night or by day, and it was not necessary to go close to it to get a view, for one could look down on it from the hillside streets of the island.

One could cross over to Kowloon and the New Territories. A considerable area of Kowloon adjacent to the sea was flat land, but it was backed by hills. The original Kowloon, still remaining, was a walled town where the last of the Sung emperors fled from the pursuing Mongol barbarians. Not so busy as Victoria, Kowloon had a fine, lengthy street, Nathan Road, through which it was a delight to stroll. Boundary Street, a couple of miles from its tip, marked the commencement of the New Territories, a mountainous region devoted to agriculture and where the farmers' way of life remained unchanged for centuries. At Castle Peak on the west coast, it was delicious to sit and watch the junks returning in the evenings, the golden sunlight glinting on the sails and dancing on the blue water of the bay. At Shatin was a noted monastery known as the Ten Thousand Buddhas Monastery, located on a hill, and devotees had to climb innumerable steps to reach it. The so-called Amah Rock in this area was supposed to be the metamorphosis of a woman vainly watching for the return of her husband, a fisherman.

The conflict was ravaging its neighbor, China, which was engaged in a life-and-death struggle against the brutal assault of a militaristic power, and affected Hong Kong but mildly. Living within its peaceful confines, it was difficult to realize that not far away an epic struggle was being waged, a struggle between a poorly armed people, whose desire was to live at peace with all the world, and a horde of pillagers, insensate with the fury of militarism. The ceaseless streams of refugees from ruined cities—from Shanghai, Amoy, and Canton—formed the principal reminder of the war. The population rose to over a million and a half, and houses became congested. Destitute were many of these unfortunate refugees, as they fled pell-mell out of occupied territory. The many movements underway to collect funds for the Chinese cause also served to bring home the reality of war to rich and poor alike.

When the next scene in the tragedy opened, when the deluge swept over the European continent, Hong Kong naturally came to be officially at war with Nazi Germany, whose criminal action in attacking Poland lifted the curtain. But the island was too far away for Hitler even to dream of molding its destiny. It maintained the even tenor of its existence with hardly any change.

No doubt that existence was somewhat precarious. At any moment a fit of madness might seize the despoiler of the East and precipitate an attack. The colony was, as it were, perched on the brim of a volcano liable to be engulfed by boiling torrents of lava. The inhabitants lived in an atmosphere of illusive security, though they knew well enough their danger. At times excitement rose to fever pitch and nerves were strained. Several times the assault seemed imminent. On the evening when news reached Hong Kong of the fall of Canton, when the papers issued a special edition to announce the fact, war was brought perilously close. After the unexpected collapse of France, the Japanese assumed an exceedingly arrogant attitude. Being the opportunists they were, they massed troops on the border and threatened to launch their invasion. The populace thought that zero hour had come, and a deathly silence reigned in the city. The booking offices of the shipping companies were crowded, those who could afford it fleeing over the waters to a haven of refuge. Strangely enough, when the bomb actually burst, the inhabitants least expected it. After so many false alarms, they found it difficult to believe that this time it was true. In spite of repeated counsel from the government urging evacuation, few people departed.

The life of the students at Hong Kong University was enviable. Established by the public, with aid from the government, this institution of higher learning was designed to promote cultural understanding between East and West. From the start, it was intended not just to serve the local populace but also to contribute to the cause of education in general. Its nucleus was the Hong Kong Medical College, from which Dr. Sun Yat-sen, the founder of the Republic of China, was the first to graduate. It attracted Chinese persons and those of other races from all over the Far East, from China, Annam, Java, and more especially from Malaya, which, including Singapore, contributed more than a third of the total number of names in the enrollment register in 1941.

The buildings occupied elevated ground in Pokfulam in the western suburbs of the city. The main buildings were located near the road, while the houses of the staff and most of the hostels were constructed at a higher level. Three of the hostels were run by the university and were built on terraces cut out of the hillside; they were placed one below the other. The highest was May Hall, named after a former governor of the colony. I resided there and, from my window, I enjoyed a superb view of the city below, the gleaming sea and its ships, and Kowloon, backed by towering peaks, softly blue in the distance. It was good exercise to tread the steps daily to attend lectures or go to town, but constant repetition made one fail to consider it as such; familiarity blunts perception.

The grounds with their woods and gardens, their winding and stepped paths, presented a fine spectacle. The trees and plants put forth lovely flowers, and the birds sang blithely as they flitted among the branches.

The shrill music of the cicadas sliced through the air. Owls and bats could be seen on the wing at dusk. Nothing could be more enchanting than standing at some vantage point at twilight and seeing the day fade to its close. The golden light lingered on the trees while birds slowly wheeled in the sky above. The shadows lengthened, and one walked away in a mood of serenity, joy, and pensiveness.

The principal worry of the students was not imminent war but the imminent examinations. They were for the most part zealous in the prosecution of their studies, doubtless actuated by a worthy desire to enter the heaven of scholastic knowledge but just as certainly by the threat of sitting in anguish in the hell of failure at the annual tussle. When the critical period was due, a profound hush fell over the hostels. Soon after the meals were over, each person could be found in his cubicle, buried deep in his books and notes. They burned the midnight oil or, rather, consumed more watts of electrical energy far into the night, endeavoring to keep themselves awake by imbibing prodigious amounts of potent coffee. They were not interested in Hitler's stagy perorations, nor were they even remotely curious about Japanese culture.

Outside their academic studies they held debates, attended social functions, and played games. They were fond of Hollywood movies and loved to sing snatches of popular tunes, the more inane the more popular. The Great Hall of the university, besides being used for examinations, congregations, and meetings, held many a concert and not a few dramatic performances. The students naturally were not in receipt of incomes earned by themselves but depended on their families; still, out of their pocket money, they contributed to the China Medical Relief Fund.

Their life centered around the hostels, which provided them with the requisite opportunities for social intercourse. Lasting friendships were formed and minds were broadened by the exchange of views. Lively debate, rational and not so rational, was frequent on any and every subject. The center of each hostel was its club located in a large hall on the ground floor, where the students spent most of their leisure hours. They might read newspapers and magazines, gather around the chess table, play endless games of table tennis, listen to the radio, turn on the gramophone, or simply indulge in free and easy conversation. Thus did their lives flow serenely until all of a sudden they were engulfed in the maelstrom of war.

2. Those Eighteen Fateful Days

On the morning of December 8, 1941, at about eight o'clock, loud explosions were heard. Rushing to the veranda, I looked in the direction of Kowloon, whence volumes of smoke rose to the skies. Kai Tak Airport was being bombed: the war in Hong Kong had begun. Our surprise and consternation could well be imagined, as we were absolutely unprepared for it, in spite of the fact that for the past few days there was an atmosphere of tension and speculation concerning the probable commencement of hostilities. But the students, like the populace in general, did not take the signs seriously, and they were imbued with the belief that the crisis would blow off as usual. Not one of them had taken his departure from the colony. In fact, as it was examination time, they were studying hard.

The duration of the first raid amounted to only a few minutes. There was quite a number of people who, for hours afterward, continued to labor under the illusion that it was an air-raid practice carried out by British planes. Recently there had been an increasing number of such practices, though not, to my recollection, any accompanied by explosions. However, the inhabitants quickly adapted themselves to the new conditions and evinced few signs of hysteria. Other raids followed on that day, and fires from bombed buildings were visible. The government maintained internal order, and looting was kept well under control. Kitchens were speedily established for the distribution of rice to the needy in certain places, like the Central Market on Queen's Road. The streets became comparatively deserted.

The enemy navy effectively sealed the island, and all neutral shipping was peremptorily ordered to scamper off its waters within thirty-six hours. An army from Kwangtung came to invade the colony. It approached from the direction of Shumchun just over the border and, for the first few days until the evacuation of Kowloon, hostilities on the island itself were confined to the increasingly frequent air raids, which wrought damage to civilian life and property. Kowloon was abandoned on the fourth day of the war, and the siege of the island began. Everybody was well aware that, whatever might be its immediate future, the ultimate destiny of this small stretch of territory would not hang on the battle now raging within its borders. Hence, all were voracious for news of other areas of combat, and any misfortunes that might befall them now were borne as stoically as the circumstances would permit.

As for the students, most of them were enrolled either in the local volunteer force or in the various civil defense services, such as the Air Raid Precautions, the First Aid Service, the Auxiliary Fire Brigade, or the Food Control Department. On that very Monday when peace was shattered, the university immediately terminated its studies, and some of its buildings were changed into a relief hospital, receiving civilian casualties. Many of the students continued to reside in the hostels, as it was difficult for them to find accommodation elsewhere since they were coming from overseas. Though their prospects seemed blasted and the outlook was bleak, they did not make any complaints. As for me, I became an air-raid warden, stationed around the university grounds.

After the occupation of Kowloon, hostilities temporarily died down to minor proportions as the Japanese were bringing up their forces. From the morning of the fifteenth, a general attack was launched against the island after the government unhesitatingly rejected their demand a couple of days earlier for surrender of the island. When they dispatched another request of the like nature on the seventeenth, it again met with the same firm refusal. During these brief intervals, when the enemy expected negotiations to be under way and ceased firing their cannons, a peculiar quiet hovered uneasily over the beleaguered island. Barbed-wire barricades were set up along the waterfront. Once so prosperously busy with bustling humanity, it was now a scene of destruction. The contending forces erected artillery on both sides of the harbor, and throughout the day and night the whiz of shellfire could be heard. In the Causeway Bay and Shaukiwan areas, bombs set alight fires that blazed for days, and at North Point petrol tanks were shelled and set aflame. In return, on the Kowloon side, after being struck by shells, godowns in Mongkok sent forth their glow into the sky. What a sight these fires were at night, leaping tongues, blood red against the dark sky! In the daytime dense clouds of black smoke floated and rolled in various directions.

Planes bombed the stricken city several times a day, and they were not opposed by any fighter aircraft, only by ack-ack guns. Scrupulousness about objectives was absent. Shrapnel and splinters flew like arrows in all directions, wounding and killing at random. If not for the excellent air-raid shelters, the casualties would undoubtedly have been considerably higher. A great many people, including whole families, made permanent abodes of these places, removing their beds and sleeping there at night. A friend of mine spent so many hours in these gloomy tunnels that he was quite thrilled when he occasionally emerged into the bright light of day. How often did I see shrapnel fly into doorways, houses in populous districts reduced to ruins with volumes of smoke billowing upward, or the injured being carried into ambulances! Once very early in the war, while I was standing on a road in Happy Valley near the ARP headquarters, a plane circled low overhead, and immediately afterward a loud explosion burst in the vicinity; a building was destroyed and the window panes in other houses shivered to pieces. Among the casualties was a girl who died instantaneously from a cracked head.

The planes came frequently, almost on the heels of the sirens, which shrieked so many times a day that the signals seemed to lose all significance. Later, when the electric supply failed, the sirens ceased to sound. The planes did not fly in close formation, but each wound its own way so as to avoid making a single target for the antiaircraft batteries. They did not merely let loose their loads of bombs but indulged in machine-gunning just as readily. They never, however, came at night, which was rent only by the sound of cannon fire from both sides. No one ventured into the streets when dusk descended, for curfews were on and blackouts continued every night. We slept uneasily in the dark, listening to the firing, and in our meditations finding whatever consolation we could.

I was aware that a historical event was taking place. As I walked the streets, I saw some of the scenes unfolding that contributed to the making of the drama: the dropping of bombs clattering and screaming in their gravitational flight, the formations of planes circling unopposed and operated by men who presumably felt themselves in the ascendant, the buildings wrapped in flames and smoke, sandbags, pillboxes, and barricades, the dead and dying strewn about the roads—all this did not spell a workaday street scene. I was filled with sadness. I experienced no excitement, only disgust at the huge senselessness of the whole thing. This might be history but it was the kind that disgraced its pages.

What thoughts surged through my brain! Wars in history may seem romantic, as events in the past always do. One day in the distant future, even this bitter cataclysm in which I was now involved might assume rosy hues and evoke a thrill at the recollection. Herein lies the alchemy of memory. Like a picture, which charms us with its representation of a beautiful scene because it leaves out all the sordid details, memory does not reproduce an experience in its totality. By its selective art it captures for retention only certain aspects. At that time, while the experience was being forged, I felt an overwhelming sense of boredom, and I found no shred of romance in this nightmarish and unnecessary melodrama.

I reflected on the course of events and the poor control one had over one's life. Here was a city with its myriad of individual lives, each spinning out its own thread, each with its joys and sorrows, its hopes and fears. One day there was merriment; the next came the terrible sounds of war. Suddenly the million people were engulfed in one idea—possible death soon. All other pursuits, thoughts, and plans seemed irrelevant, to no purpose. One's entire tenor of life was wrecked and one's world lay in ruins.

Such thoughts crossed my mind as I lay sleeping with some other persons on the floor of what was the sitting room of the quarters of one of our former professors. I had left May Hall temporarily when I took up duty as an air-raid warden. The night was cold, and I was lying close to the electric hearth, which did not shed much warmth. Now and then came the whiz of shellfire. Suddenly there was a loud explosion. We started up and rushed to the window. A building had been hit, and fire rose to the dark sky. After some time the red glow died down. There were several other fires in the distance, but they did not draw much attention, for we had become inured to them. So easily did our minds adjust to circumstances; the unusual had become the usual, and what was horrifying had ceased to shock overmuch.

Packed like sardines, fifty students slept in one big room in the Fung Ping Shan Library. Most just spread their blankets on the floor; some made their beds on a table. As there was no light, they all retired at about six o'clock, and the sounds of conversation punctuated the darkness. Many of them first saw Hong Kong only a few months before. Destiny had played them an odd trick. They came across the sea to revel in the wonders of a strange place; wonders did they meet but of an unexpected variety. Besides the lack of light there was hardly any water, which occasionally came in drops through the only tap available. When a bomb exploded not so far away, the roof rattled as if it would crash down. The clock on the tower of the main university building stopped functioning owing to the vibrations, and its faces cracked.

As we were not at the center of events, our information gathered from various sources was by no means reliable. A good deal was rumor and conjecture. The uncertainty, of course, only served to engender disquiet. The government released untrue news for the purpose of bolstering the morale of the populace or for upholding its own prestige. The most distressing rumors were those that concerned the landing of the enemy on the island. Very early in the war we had already heard of successful landings, and as the conflict continued we got more and more stories of raging battles and masses of corpses. Now they were in North Point, now in Aberdeen, now in Wanchai, now in Happy Valley, now in Repulse Bay; there was hardly a place where at some time or other there wasn't a rumor of a landing. Sometimes we even fancied that the ubiquitous Japanese had suddenly appeared right in front of us. We were, in fact, living in a nightmare.

On the streets a common sight was people hurrying along with their belongings to places, which, for the time being, they thought comparatively safer. Poor victims! Many of them might have seen war before, for the colony was swollen with refugees from the Chinese provinces, but most of them had hitherto only heard of it or seen it on the screen. Those who had were undergoing it afresh, and those who hadn't now knew its horrors firsthand.

As the war progressed, godowns containing food supplies were annihilated. The power station was shelled and electricity vanished. Water ceased to come through the taps. Roads were severely damaged and transport made difficult. As food stocks were not concentrated in one or two places, their loss was partial and did not spell disaster. The cynically minded might point out that the enforced cessation of the electric supply meant automatic blackouts at night, thus saving the police and the populace a lot of trouble, for it was said that the police had been known to fire into a house where lights were not dimmed. Now we realized the virtues of candles and oil lamps. The unavailability of water from taps was a greater nuisance, but as it could be drawn from wells, we survived. Ruts and craters in the roads were no hindrance to pedestrian traffic.

The Japanese resorted to psychological warfare by posing as champions of the Chinese. Their leaflets proclaimed that the British in their century-old occupation of Hong Kong had cruelly maltreated the Chinese and now they, the Japanese, were out to recover the territory on behalf of the Chinese and avenge the disgrace. The people were asked to massacre the foreigners to terminate the war. However, the appeal did not work, as the propaganda was so crude, so devoid of subtlety, that it could not mislead a simpleton.

The Chungking government kept a contingent of secret police in Hong Kong. They were instructed to cooperate with the colonial government. They were in contact with secret societies that were illegal and that were now asked to take part in the struggle against the invaders. Without their help, the gangsters might have been tempted to rise up and murder some of the Westerners, not due to propaganda leaflets dropped from Japanese aircraft, but on their own account, for they had no reason to love the British who had always endeavored to suppress them. They aided in the capture of fifth columnists and saboteurs, who were shot under the martial law in force during the hostilities. They were useful in preventing disorder, and they helped in curbing looting, which, if not rigorously controlled, would have assumed frightful dimensions.

The Japanese made several attempts to land on the island, but they did not succeed until the night of the eighteenth, when they crossed the harbor under cover of their fire. Once they had effected a landing, the situation rapidly deteriorated. They were veterans, well armed, highly mobile, skilful in night warfare, and led by officers who knew what they wanted, and they had planes to aid them. On the other hand, the British had some raw troops, especially the Canadians, and they had no air force. The enemy swiftly captured other parts of the island as the British, who had never fought the Japanese before and had a low opinion of their military prowess, were probably taken by surprise and became demoralized.

The populace tried to keep up their morale by pinning their faith to reports that troops sent by Chungking were on their way to succor them. When the Chinese government had been in no position to prevent its coastal cities from falling into the hands of the enemy, it was very odd to expect it to be able to overcome them in Hong Kong. But right up to the end people were still looking forward to the troops and wondering why they hadn't arrived yet. The government was the origin of the belief. Broadcasts by the BBC in England were received eagerly, but what the listeners got was propaganda that gave an untrue picture of the war and only made them laugh with dismay.

Stories trickled in of Japanese brutality, stories that made the blood of many listeners curdle. Three enemy soldiers, it was said, who were lurking in a hill to which they had retreated, descended at night on a house in Happy Valley in search of food. When the inmates, on opening the door, found themselves confronted with the unaccustomed spectacle of fierce soldiers with bayonets, they trembled violently. One was a fortune-teller who, imagining that the best way to mollify these unwelcome visitors was to load them with praises, hesitatingly advanced and started to tell their fortunes, predicting for them a glorious, resplendent future. All members of his profession are conspicuously voluble and, impelled by fear, he waxed eloquent. Unluckily for him, the soldiers did not understand a word of what he was speaking in Cantonese (few people in Hong Kong could carry on a conversation in Japanese, and the soldiers of the volcanic isles understood no language save their own). The intruders ended his discourse by bayoneting him, following it up by killing all the residents—men, women, and children—more than a score in all. One person, however, who was tossed aside after receiving a bayonet thrust (which was not serious) escaped to tell the story.

All sorts of other atrocities were reported of them and, while some might not be true, much was genuine. Stories of bayoneting of men and raping of women were all too common, and they were calculated to unsettle one's mind. People were afraid to think of the morrow, and they had no means of escape from the beleaguered island, in which there was not a single spot where they could retire for real safety, where they would not have to face the savages. They shivered for their property, for their lives, for their wives and daughters. Gloom, unutterable gloom, and dread clutched at the heart, whispering incessantly!

Many students narrowly escaped death. One was driving a truck, and, unaware that the enemy had effected a landing on the island, rushed right into their lines and found himself a prisoner. He was propelled into a wooden shed where he found a number of air-raid wardens who had been arrested around that area. They were kept there the whole night wondering about the outcome of their misadventure. The next morning, when the British trained their guns on that region, the shed was as likely as not to be hit. The Japanese sentry on duty, not relishing the prospect of becoming a casualty, ran away, leaving the prisoners to their fate. They frantically burst open the door and escaped from their perilous position.

War raged on the streets in the suburbs, and on the twenty-third, in a counterattack, part of the forces of the foe was driven back. The gratifying news raised the depressed spirits of the populace—but only for a short time. The invaders augmented their troops and the tragedy drew to a close. On the twenty-fifth, the sound of fire was less intense, and as the day advanced we were surprised at the profound quiet, which had suddenly alighted on the place. Perhaps it was a temporary truce, as had happened before; most believed that, it being Christmas Day, the attackers and defenders had agreed to a brief respite. Pathetic indeed was the conjecture! In fact, the enemy had landed such an overwhelming number of troops that resistance would have been futile. To prevent further atrocities the government decided to surrender, and the governor crossed over to Kowloon to put a stop to the fighting. I did not know of it until shortly after five o'clock in the evening when—waiting for a friend, Hung Shek Chiu, in his house—he came running in breathlessly to announce the news. I immediately emerged into the streets. People were hurrying they knew not whither, and houses were rapidly bolted and barred.

Thus fell Hong Kong, its hundred years of growing prosperity and radiant peace terminating in bloodshed and anguish. Only a while ago its centenary was greeted with acclamations, but now ruin stared it in the face. Its collapse in the short space of eighteen days bred immense consternation and was difficult to believe. How did it happen? The people, who had never previously entertained any presentiment of such a catastrophe, surmised only for a short while, as there were more urgent problems to occupy their minds.

3. Under Japanese Rule

The first night of the surrender of Hong Kong seemed strange and brought dreadful forebodings. Though Kowloon had by that time passed under the rule of the invaders for a fortnight, the islanders were ignorant of its treatment and its present circumstances; they did not know what the men of ill repute would do in the first flush of victory. Half a month of terrifying sounds was succeeded by a night of more terrifying silence.

When the morrow broke, all shops were closed and some time elapsed before people dared to stir out of their houses. Tin hats and gas masks hastily discarded by their possessors were piled in heaps. The streets were filthy with mounds of uncleared rubbish, and burst sewers rendered the air of some roads impossible to breathe. Unlike human beings, flies thrived, swarms of them flying about gorging themselves. All motorcars were commandeered, and those not required were deposited in places such as the racecourse.

The original police force had been retained to maintain order, but they were armed only with cudgels. Looters performed their fell work on a rampant scale. Bands of robbers infested the streets and alleys and divested pedestrians of whatever was on their person. They broke into houses in a systematic manner. They would call on a peaceable abode and shout to the residents to open the door; if this was not immediately done, they broke it down and demanded the surrender of money and jewelry. If the householder was to bargain with them, alleging that he had in his possession only such and such a sum of money, if it seemed tempting enough they would agree to accept a certain amount and depart precipitately in order that they might not lose any precious time in pillaging other houses. If, on the contrary, it was affirmed that there was no cash on the premises, they ravenously ransacked every nook and corner, carrying away every dollar and jewel they could ferret out. After they had wrought their will elsewhere they came back again, this time in search of clothing and easily portable articles. They would return a third time to cart away the furniture. Different bands of looters might raid the same building.

The Japanese stationed sentries on every street, ostensibly to keep order and prevent looting, but really to intimidate everybody. Looters, as well as those whom they pretended to be such, were arrested and tied with ropes to trees and posts, with long strips of white cloth attached to them on which were written their crimes. They were thus kept for a day for public exhibition before they were shot. I once saw a youth allegedly caught for such a crime kneeling in the center of a street with a Japanese soldier standing by; a crowd surged some distance away, among them the criminal's mother wailing loudly. Trucks drove along the streets piled high with corpses in all conditions of horror. The principal work of the sentries was to salute their officers and, as compensation, to demand that passersby bow to them meekly. I noticed a feeble, old gentleman who, passing a sentry's post and being confronted with the need to perform this ceremony, endeavored to bow while sitting in a sedan-chair, as he was unable to stand; the sentry dragged him down forcibly and gave him a thundering slap.

The soldiers summarily killed those engaged in looting and took to the same alluring job themselves. Pedestrians were stopped and deprived of their watches and fountain pens, for which they possessed a penchant. They invaded houses and seized whatever appealed to their fancy. Whereas many buildings had their doors so stoutly constructed or so securely locked and barricaded that ordinary looters found themselves baffled, now every house was open to them, for none dared disobey their commands to let them enter the place. Whereas ordinary looters seldom resorted to physical violence and wrought injury and death, the same could not be said of their indefatigable imitators in uniform. They did not always enter in search of lifeless property though; they often came in quest of girls, living property to them.

The conquerors set about organizing a new government: after skilful destruction came bungling construction. They chose hotels and banks wherein to improvise their offices. Their headquarters were located in the Peninsula Hotel in Kowloon before removal to the building of the Hong Kong and Shanghai Banking Corporation in Victoria. The employees of the fallen colonial government were recalled to work mainly at their old jobs. One of the new government's first acts was to proclaim an edict calling on the population to cooperate in ushering in a new era of peace and prosperity and announcing pardon to all those who repented of their past misdeeds, including the supporters of the Chungking. regime. It seemed that they had no quarrel with the Chinese (though they were fighting China and had been fanatically, exclusively concentrating on it for more than four years), but only with the British and Americans.

About three hundred prominent merchants were ordered to form an association for the rehabilitation of the captured territory and, trembling for their property, they hastened to execute their masters' instructions. These so-called representatives of the Chinese community might be able to save themselves but could certainly do nothing for the welfare of the people.

Enemy aliens—that is, the British, Americans, and Dutch—who were not military personnel, were at first loosely confined to places, like hotels in the Wanchai area, and it was not until late January that they were sent to the internment camp at Stanley. The staff of the university continued to live in their quarters and were among the last to be interned.

The commercial prosperity of the colony was as much in ruins as the bombed buildings. Shops and companies could not resume business, for their capital, which was kept in the banks, was not forthcoming (to say nothing of their losses during and after the war due to bombs and looting and the lack of an adequate market). Later, only 5 percent of the deposits were returned with the result that the rich found themselves enmeshed in bankruptcy. As if this was not enough, notes of denominations of more than ten dollars ceased to be legal tender. A black market sprang up, in which they might be exchanged for small notes at a rate varying at different times from half to three-quarters of their nominal value. The worthless military yen, which was originally fixed with respect to the Hong Kong dollar at one to two, was forcibly put into circulation. When first issued, it was made available to the public at places of exchange set up for the purpose, but hardly any person wanted it. The ruling was then made that shipping and bus fares as well as rice obtained from government centers must be paid for in it; furthermore, in respect of water, electricity, and telephone services, fresh deposits were required and revised charges were made, all much higher than before, and payment must also be in it. The consequence was that there was a rush for it and queues were formed outside the exchange offices.

Famine reared its Gorgon's head and the streets were strewn with the dead and dying. It was horrifying to walk along the pavement and observe stiff, ghastly corpses, and more nerve-racking still to notice the dying, piteously holding out their writhing hands to passersby or breathing their last breath, the agonies of death rattling in their throats. Beggars were so numerous that the natural human feelings of sympathy in bystanders seemed frozen; they even stretched themselves in the middle of lanes, crying loudly in such a monstrous state of raggedness and filth that one could not but blush with shame and indignation at the thought that men could be reduced to something worse than pigs. Later, the authorities experimented with frantic attempts to make the city assume an aspect of greater prosperity by rounding up these paupers at night and removing them to some desolate region, where they were abandoned to die en masse or, so it was said, were just dumped into the sea like so much rubbish. But a fortnight after one such drastic sweep, another crop was sure to emerge just as prolific so that the streets were never actually free from them.

Then there were the girls who sprouted up in doorways in the main streets to become birds of the night. The fact that so many recruits were suddenly drawn into the oldest profession in the world was eloquent testimony of the circumstances of the time. There were also the gambling dens that sprang into existence overnight; it was strange that when people had no money to buy food they had plenty to throw away.

A most annoying phenomenon conducted in the streets was the search for concealed weapons on the person. At countless places, passersby had to submit to this indignity. Those who intended to board the ferry launches could not escape it at the piers. Trams and buses were stopped and all the passengers had to alight. Besides certain fixed stations where one knew after one or two experiences what to expect, search parties would suddenly swoop down on a spot one day to vanish to another the next. This probe, sometimes undertaken by the Japanese sentries themselves but more often by the policemen under their supervision (the police were the most obnoxious of all, the traitors in the ill-starred colony), was carried out in no gentle manner. The women suffered most, the searchers passing their hands over their bosoms in an indelicate sort of way. One girl, who was searched by a policeman in a more than usually outrageous manner, unable to restrain her indignation, inflicted on him a good slap; the gendarme standing by dispatched her to the police station, where her punishment is best left to the imagination. After many weeks, the burden on the feminine half of the population was supposed to be lightened when—owing to the feeble representations of the body of representatives whose wives had probably encountered the same species of treatment, for the Japanese soldiers were no respecters of persons when it came to subject races—the authorities consented to employ members of their own sex to examine them. But these women inspectors were stationed at only a few places, like the Star Ferry; elsewhere they resembled the invisible man.

Ever and anon a certain section of the town was put under curfew when barbed-wire barricades were erected and sentries with guns and bayonets strutted ferociously. For hours on end crowds waited patiently for the ban to be lifted to traverse a road in order to reach their homes. The worst of it was when those who lived on one side of the harbor found themselves on the other side, unable to catch the launches in time and were forced to pass the night at a friend's place or a hotel.

The occupied territory was divided into districts under district bureaus, whose two chief duties were the registration of the population for the rationing of rice and the issuing of permits to those who wished to return to their villages. The aim of the government, though it did not expressly state its intention, was to turn the island into a fortress and a base. As it did not want to revive its status as a commercial port, it had no use for the vast population whom it encouraged to leave. Detailed instructions were given in posters regarding the procedure for obtaining the necessary permit, the amount of luggage (two-bag limit), which each person could take with him, and the time of departure of boats for Macao, Kwangchowwan, and elsewhere. In any case, many people would have attempted to escape from what was now an inferno, but the government simplified matters by placing no restrictions on evacuation. In this its motive was not any species of benevolence, however mild, but pure expediency. No speck of anxiety tainted its heart concerning such an insignificant trifle as the livelihood of the people, who would only consume great quantities of rice and who would predictably perish in such numbers as to probably bring epidemics, which might threaten the precious lives of the members of the much vaunted Imperial Army of Dai-Nippon. Hence, the wishes of the conquerors and the conquered coincided on this one plane. The population commenced to drop rapidly. Many took the overland route, trekking over the border past Shumchun, while others left in crowded steamers for the ports, which were the gateways to the interior of China. They were all supposed to return to their villages to pursue their peaceful occupations as farmers but, of course, many established themselves instead in the cities of Free China, ardently engaged in work much less welcome to the brigands who had upset their lives.

In lonely places it was quite common for the soldiers to give free rein to their rampancy. They forcibly deprived people of their possessions, committed rape, and shot passersby on the slightest provocation. In comparatively busy streets, they controlled themselves somewhat and confined themselves to slapping those who roused their ire or apprehending them and dispatching them to the nearest police station to be maltreated. Sometimes the scene appeared farcical. Once I saw a short soldier who was manning a sentry's post jumping up and down to slap a tall man whose only offense was that he passed him without doffing his hat. For no rhyme or reason, a soldier would pull out his dagger and lunge even at children to demonstrate his prowess. Robbery was committed not only by individual soldiers on their own account but by the authorities who confiscated whatever goods they wanted; daily, trucks rumbled along the streets fully loaded with such commodities.

There was no lack of collaborators. However, the majority were merely ordinary folk out to get jobs and make a living. It would be too much to expect the average person to prefer to die of heroic starvation rather than serve the government of the day, however bad it might be. They might be those compelled to work for the enemy against their will for fear of consequences. The truly obnoxious collaborators were those who went out of the way to gain the favor of their masters by acting as informers and advisers, enabling them to injure their compatriots more effectively or to consolidate their power more strongly. Such traitors launched newspapers to sing the praises of the new masters and do propaganda on their behalf. One of these inglorious, enterprising newspapers, strangely enough, one day carried the news that the Japanese conquered Hong Kong on behalf of China and they would place it under the jurisdiction of the Nanking government of Wang Ching-wei. The Japanese were by no means pleased with this and shut down the paper in question.

For many days the main trade was confined to roadside stalls, which sprouted up like mushrooms on every street and which sold all sorts of commodities, the most conspicuous item being canned foods. Prices quadrupled over their pre-war levels. There was a great shortage of rice, and people cut down on their meals and took it in the more economical form of gruel. Restaurants did not go out of existence, but few were able to provide rice meals. One oddity, which I had never seen previously but which became quite common, was the spectacle of a customer surreptitiously rising up and running away without paying the bill and the proprietor chasing after him.

I continued to stay in May Hall together with other overseas students. There was a stock of foodstuff consisting mainly of rice, soybeans, and canned goods. The students formed a committee that arranged the distribution of meals. Day after day we had boiled soybeans until I swore that if I survived the war I would never touch this legume for the rest of my life. However, this strong resolution has been weakly maintained, for I can still relish it. On Chinese New Year's Eve the students even organized a party at the hostel, the chief item being a supper in addition to music, dancing, and games. The way they enjoyed themselves was pathetic. Merriment is never so merry and miserable as when set against a background of misery. The weather appeared singularly cold, possibly owing to the dismal conditions.

The students looked like lost sheep, wandering around the university grounds, loitering in the buildings, or sitting in their rooms disconsolately discussing their predicament. One evening a group of us were sitting on the grass and whiling away our time chattering.

"This is ironical," said Wong Meng Tuck, an engineering student. "My father wanted me to study in England, but I preferred Hong Kong. And now here I am sitting on the grass."

"My case is the opposite," intervened Lim Geok Huat, a medical student. "I preferred to study at the Singapore Medical College, but my father considered that out here I could get a degree instead of merely a diploma, and now I have neither."

"I don't know why I ever came here," remarked Chew Siu Lan, a female student in the arts faculty. "I wonder how I am going to return to my home in Negri Sembilan."

"Very little chance," remarked Geok Huat. "It's improbable there will be any shipping service to Malaya."

"What are we going to do then?" asked Siu Lan wistfully.

"We carry on from day to day and see what happens," said Lily Chow, another female student of arts. "It's difficult to know what to do. It's so confusing."

"I know what I am going to do," said Goh Boon Seng, who had come to the university only a few months ago. "I am going to China."

"Do you know anybody in China?" I asked.

"No," he replied, "but I don't suppose I'll starve to death."

"It can't be worse than lingering here," said Geok Huat. "At any rate, we'll be free. Here we are living under military tyranny. Every miserable soldier can lord it over us. You know, I was coming up the steps from Lyttelton Road yesterday when I passed a sentry. There was no soldier there before and I wasn't paying attention to my surroundings. Suddenly a slap stung my face, and the next moment the wretch drew his dagger and lunged at me. I was petrified with terror."

"Luckily he didn't kill you," said Lily Chow with concern. "What was your crime?"

"Blessed if I know," was the reply.

"I presume you didn't bow to His Highness," I interposed.

"I had a nasty experience too," said Meng Tuck. "I was walking along Chater Road about a week ago when three Japanese officers rode past in single file on horseback. For some unknown reason, when the last horse was near me, it reared its front legs and neighed. Its rider apparently considered that I was responsible for this. He raised his whip and lashed at me. Fortunately it only hit me on the leg."

"These fellows think no end of themselves," said Boon Seng angrily. "I feel sick merely looking at them."

"I don't know why we are so unfortunate as to have to meet with war," remarked Lily Chow. "We used to read about it happening in other places and I couldn't for the life of me understand why people should fight."

Her words reminded me of Kaspar in Southey's poem: *But what they fought each other for I could not well make out.* However, I felt too depressed to make a humorous allusion.

"I never thought I would be caught in a stricken city," said Siu Lan.

"I did not realize the Japanese were so strong," said Boon Seng. "When they could not conquer a single country like China, which was weak militarily and had been experiencing civil war and foreign exploitation, it was amazing that they should have even thought of attacking so many territories simultaneously."

"I don't suppose they will be able to get away with it in the end," I said. "We can look forward to happier days."

"I trust you are right," said Siu Lan, who looked on the verge of tears. "But in the meantime I am living in a nightmare."

"What are you talking so solemnly about?" inquired a newcomer who was strolling toward us.

"What do you think?" countered Geok Huat. "Could we be discussing sports, parties, picnics?"

"Our old life appears so far away," said Meng Tuck, "like a dream. But it's better not to think of it or we'll be unable to stand our present ordeal. Our most urgent problem is to survive. It's getting dark. Let's go in."

4. Exclusive Exploitation Sphere

The Japanese were indubitably fond of slogans that were such nonsense that one didn't know whether to laugh or cry. The island was pasted all over with their tripe. The walls of fine buildings were desecrated with posters, and over the streets were hung horizontal strips of cloth bearing the same pernicious characters. The wretched newspapers wrote commentaries on them.

Of all their slogans, which were manufactured as though with the aid of a distorting mirror whereby an ordinary figure becomes a grotesque image, the most persistent and egregious was the notorious "East Asia Co-Prosperity Sphere." After bandying it in China for years with results about as pitiable as those of a candidate who has forfeited his deposit in an election, they now tried its effect in Hong Kong, for somehow failure could never convince them of its vacuity. They seemed unable to understand that they could propagandize but could not induce belief, just as they could conquer but could not enforce submission. Immediately after the occupation, the inhabitants were invited to participate zealously in the noble task of constructing this sphere. Hong Kong was a great city, now magnanimously invested with this wondrous duty. To achieve this great goal, the Imperial Army wished to shatter American and British Power. The Chinese were not to worry about their lives and property, for they were under its benevolent protection.

It was marvelous that there was such generosity on the part of the Japanese that they were quite willing to lose their lives, waste their substance, and incur hatred in order to bring prosperity to peoples who did not appreciate the sacrifice. Occasionally there might be a sage or hero willing to undergo suffering for the sake of others, but here was a nation full of heroes who—to their chagrin, like so many other martyrs—evoked no admiration. Perhaps this was but natural for, if persons who became martyrs had been accorded the rightful recognition for their work, they would not have been made such. It was a fact, though it was unfortunate for the conquerors that people generally failed to understand their good intentions.

Whether anybody was truly deceived by their preposterous palaver about the co-prosperity of the two races is doubtful. Manifestly, there was no deficiency of traitors who, for their own private benefit, were not loath to follow their masters in mechanical repetition of meaningless terms. But if they sincerely believed in their validity, they must have been fools. Again, in every piece of occupied territory, there was bound to be a large class of temporizers who, living there at the time of its fall, passively acquiesced in their fate and paid lip service to the conquerors. Their attitude was not heroic, but it could hardly be designated as one of genuine treachery. They were of no particular use to the new government, which could put no trust in them.

In its practical manifestation, "co-prosperity" euphemistically denoted "exclusive exploitation." In the eyes of the ruling class of Japan, Asian countries were subject to exploitation by both native and Western governments and capitalists. Such a deplorable state of affairs must be rectified by the chosen people of Amaterasu Omikami, the Goddess of the Sun. Foreign influence must be banished from Asia, native governments destroyed, and native capitalists ruined. What would remain would be vast expanses of fertile land containing valuable resources and an obedient class of slaves. Under their tyrannical rule, these resources would be exclusively appropriated for the use of the Japanese government. Such was their intention, and anybody could divine it unhesitatingly.

Sun Yat-sen, the founder of the Chinese Republic, stated that China was a semicolony, subject to international control. Japan's aim was to improve on this by transforming it into a real colony. One who was at all cognizant of the evolution of Korea into a completely subservient land, passing through the chrysalis stage of dependent independence, could not but know that if Japan were ultimately to emerge victorious, even the puppet governments of Pu Yi and Wang Ching-wei—keeping up an appearance of Manchuria and China being still ruled by their own people—would eventually be abolished. There would be direct government from Tokyo through the medium of Japanese governors. The officials in these countries would all be Japanese. The puppets, who at that time seemed quite happy in their coveted posts, would find themselves without a job.

Besides its exclusive character, the exploitation of the predatory hordes was unlimited. No restrictions were placed on their appetites; insatiability was their watchword. While people were perishing like flies in the streets of Hong Kong, rice and other foodstuffs were being transported out of the land. Anything that they needed was taken away, such as medical supplies and electronic apparatuses, and even the railings of buildings were melted down in order to get iron. It is superfluous to mention that, as in the cities of China, machinery of all descriptions was promptly shipped away.

The oddity was that they seemed to need everything. Libraries, including the university libraries, were ransacked for books, especially those dealing with the Pacific, Australia, the East Indies, the Indo-Chinese Peninsula, and India. They had a special department for this purpose located in the building of the former National City Bank of New York. Here, books were sorted, packed in wooden cases, and forwarded to Tokyo, which apparently was designed to be a revival of Ancient Rome, into which poured the spoils from conquered countries. A profound contempt had these islanders for other races, but they did not extend it to the creations of their brains and hands; they could find a use for everything others produced.

What the government needed it took by force. The occupants of mansions were peremptorily turned out onto the street at short notice in order that troops might find suitable accommodation. Furniture was not to be removed; in fact, everything was to be left behind except clothing. In a few cases, after the departure of the troops, the houses were returned to their owners, who came back to find only bleak walls and floors strewn with litter. An entire area, comprising five busy streets in Wanchai, was cleared of all its former inhabitants for the use of Japanese civilians who were to have it as their commercial center.

Labor was conscripted, or else advantage was taken of starvation to recruit workers from whom every ounce of strength was sweated out. Even under torrents of rain, gangs of coolies were to be seen dragging along heavy carts by means of ropes tied to their bodies. Wages remained unpaid until April when, after receiving for months on end scanty rations of rice with no other foodstuff, diseases such as beriberi began to attack the workers.

The soldiers did to individuals what the government did to the community as a whole. In the early days of the occupation, they were robbers pure and simple. But later, when the city was supposed to have settled down into some sort of order and shops had resumed business, they made a show of payment, though this did not always happen. A soldier might stand gazing at the shop window of a watchmaker until some good watch caught his fancy. The listed price—say, of a Cyma watch—was two hundred yen. This queer customer offered ten yen. The proprietor would pathetically protest that this was far too little, so the customer would write on a piece of paper some Chinese characters that, translated literally, meant: "Good friend, twelve yen." (The Japanese conversed with the Chinese on paper by the use of the Chinese ideograms.) By this the shopkeeper was to understand that the soldier was his good friend and, as such, he should obligingly accept twelve yen as the price. The proprietor would then write to intimate that he would go bankrupt if he took such a sum, but he was willing to receive 190 yen. This kind of bargaining would continue for half an hour until the sheet of paper was filled with words. The soldier would then write laconically: "Tomorrow come." He then went away, and the next day he duly presented himself. The same process was repeated until finally the soldier placed on the counter fourteen yen, seized the watch, and stalked off, leaving the proprietor to console himself as best he could at the loss of his helpless article.

The soldiers never failed to make their purchases in this way, forcibly seizing goods and, to keep up appearances, paying a ridiculous fraction of the actual price. If ordinary customers were charged thirty yen, they gave only one for a piece of leather that they wished to convert into a bag. Not only the soldiers but even Japanese civilians and Japanese subjects, like Formosans, virtually robbed goods in the same way, though their payments were higher. For example, at the time when eggs cost three for one Hong Kong dollar, I saw a Japanese civilian, after picking twenty-five of the choicest from a basket that belonged to an old woman, throw down three dollars and depart. Often these nominal customers went to the extent of falling into a temper because the shopkeepers did not cheerfully and immediately consent to accept the price proffered. Before leaving with the commodities, they inflicted on them a slap for what they considered their exorbitant demands.

Why the Japanese imagined that the people of Hong Kong should believe in co-prosperity is inexplicable. Their record elsewhere had not demonstrated that they cared one whit for the prosperity of those over whom they held sway. The inhabitants of Hong Kong were overwhelmingly Chinese, and it was to the Chinese that the verbal barrage of co-prosperity was directed. Why should they treat the Chinese of Hong Kong differently from those of China? And their record in China was abysmal. From the first moment of their emergence from medievalism and to evince their strength, they had picked on China as their prey. They had annexed Formosa and Korea, did whatever they could to prevent its unification and progress, set up Manchukuo, and were endeavoring to conquer the whole country. And the atrocities they had committed everywhere! What benefits had any conquered people ever derived from them?

Though the glittering comet that really lured the Japanese was territorial expansion, they were also desirous of acquiring the prestige that would attend the diffusion of their culture. To justify their aggression, conquerors commonly resort to some kind of excuse that superficially possesses a certain moral validity. An Attila indeed with barbarian pride might not need to camouflage his crime, but a modern community likes to pretend that it is brimful of intellectual and moral superiority. The diffusion of their culture by the Japanese was not a sign of their desire for the co-prosperity of the conquerors and the conquered. For example, they had compelled Formosans to accept their culture. Descendants of emigrants from the Amoy region, the younger generation of Formosans spoke Japanese and in their appearance were practically indistinguishable from their masters, but there existed not even a shadow of equality between the two races. Formosans were recruited for service in Hong Kong, but they seldom held positions higher than those of clerks. It was not difficult to perceive that there was no love lost between them and their oppressors.

It would be worth the trouble to probe a little more meticulously into this question of culture. When a nation claims the right to spread its way of life by force, it must possess transcendent qualities, it must far excel that of its neighbors, or else there would be nothing to mitigate the criminality of initiating a holocaust. If a people were raised to a much higher level of civilization, such benefit may counterbalance the loss of independence. Setting aside the narrow, regional point of view, one may find consolation in the fact that the world as a whole has made progress, that the upward trend of civilization is being maintained. When Alexander subjugated the Persian Empire, when Caesar conquered Gaul, even when the bloodthirsty Cortes eradicated the civilization of the Aztecs, a plausible case can be made out in justification of their actions. Can any plea be made for the spread of Japanese culture by force?

Originality is the characteristic of the loftiest species of intellect; discovery and invention alone make for human progress. The world would remain stagnant if it were not enriched by new ideas and products. Now the mind of the Japanese has been supinely imitative to a degree absolutely portentous and unknown to other races. Commencing from the sixth century, they emerged from barbarism by sedulously copying Chinese civilization and thereafter hardly added anything of value. Then, awakened by Western cannon, they started in the Meiji Era to learn feverishly the technical, economic, and military knowledge of Europe while retaining their social and cultural heritage for the most part. Japan stood in the limelight as a great power solely on the strength of its arms. At the outbreak of the China War, three score and ten years had elapsed since the end of the shogunate, yet this so-called great power had not made a single notable contribution in science or art, had not enriched in any way the store of human knowledge. All they had been able to do was imitate with a species of arrogant ingratitude peculiar to them. The copy could never be better than the original. Need any country go to the Japanese to learn Chinese culture or Western culture? What greater cultural prosperity could the denizens of any land obtain by its forcible incorporation into the Co-Prosperity Sphere?

5. The Ugly Face of Conquest

It would not be out of place to give a brief sketch of the principal character traits of the Japanese at that time. To themselves they were perfect and admirable. They had wondered for years why the Chinese were so reluctant to cooperate with them, racial brethren though they were. They proclaimed this relationship *ad nauseam*, this being one of the stale tricks that their propaganda experts imagined should be very effective. Unfortunately, other people's estimates of our character are so often diametrically the reverse of ours, and what seems so convincing fails to convince. No chain can bind the breeze of belief. Race is of little significance in comparison with mind, and in history fierce wars have been fought between peoples whose kinship was extremely close.

Their most outstanding trait was cruelty. Their enjoyment of suffering amounted to sadism. How often had I seen them smiling with unadulterated delight and pointing to some starving wretch, writhing on the pavement in the last stages of death! They were not sickened at the sight; they experienced not the slightest twinge of sympathy. They probably congratulated themselves that they were not reduced to such extremities.

Their irritability, bred of consciousness of power, assumed fantastic proportions. Dangling on the edge of a precipice could not be attended with more peril than walking past a sentry, as one never knew when he would resort to his favorite expression of displeasure: the slap. As a passenger, alighting from a bus to be searched, still holding between his fingers a glowing cigarette, he could bet his last dollar that he would receive this reward. If a pedestrian negligently failed to doff his hat or make a bow, if he whistled ever so low, if he did not stop with the staccato jerk of a locomotive when such an order thundered in his vicinity, the blow duly appeared like lightning. Even a smile could be misconstrued as an insult. Once, three fashionably dressed girls tripped along a pavement, giggling to themselves; across the road stood a scowling sentry who, harshly commanding them to come toward him, slapped them to their anguished surprise, as they were completely steeped in ignorance about the nature of their crime.

The slap was not the only way the soldiers expressed their displeasure and superiority. Beating with a belt or any handy instrument, pummeling with the fist, knocking down a man and sitting on him, whipping—such salutary diversions enlivened their days. They paid scant regard to distinctions between person and person. Old and young, children and adults, men and women, gentlemen and coolies—they received impartial attention.

If anything genuine ever exuded from them, it was their contempt and hatred for other races. They sincerely believed that they were descendants of celestial ancestors, members of other nations, irrespective of their rank and attainments, being equally inferior to the meanest of them. They treated those who served them almost as oppressively as those who didn't. I had even seen them cursing and browbeating police officers—their most abject slaves—in public. A policeman, stationed at a wharf to search passengers going on board vessels, bent aside twice or thrice to speak to a friend; something was evidently on his mind. A gendarme watched him a hundred paces away, strutted forward, and dealt him a resounding blow as he uttered some curses, which probably meant that the policeman was not scrupulously attentive in the discharge of his duties.

Their sense of humor leaped from the darkness of their hearts. There are varied species of humor, ranging from the sublime to the vulgar and from the refined to the coarse. The kindly exuberance of Charles Dickens and the corrective wit of George Bernard Shaw bear close affinity to beauty: they shimmer and enchant like stars. Humor is said to give a sense of balance, of proportion, but this can be true only of the normal type. If ordinary humor is not subtle, it is at least unexceptionable, and it gives piquancy to life. Unfortunately, there exists a variety of malignant humor that only serves to debase character. It is a dictum that man is the only laughing animal, but laughter can make him lower than other animals. Laughter that is aroused at the sight of pain and that finds its sweetest expression in torture should be eradicated, root and branch. The Japanese could pride themselves on their unique gift—the most degrading sense of humor imaginable. To give but a mild illustration of their perverted taste that I myself witnessed: At the pier where launches regularly left for the town of Shurnshuipo, there was always to be found collected a crowd of porters who could find no other way of earning a livelihood than by rushing forward to help the passengers carry their luggage. The gendarmes stationed there considered them a nuisance and would not permit them to approach the pier. Very often one of them would walk toward a coolie and propel him with his bayonet toward the sea, and with a sudden push of his hand tumble him over the brink. All his friends then laughed in concert at the exquisite joke and, if it happened to be early in the morning, they dubbed it a morning bath. The poor wretch had to wade with the water up to his neck toward a flight of stone steps before he could clamber out of the sea. Sometimes he was injured, with blood covering his wounded forehead, and they then laughed more heartily.

The rank and file of the army were subject to such oppression that their coarse natures could find fun only in intimidation. They thrilled at the sight of terror in others. It was very common to see them flashing their bayonets close to mere children, like the newsboys, just to hear them scream. On the morning of the third day of the occupation of the island, I was walking along a street in Sai Ying Pun, wrapped in sad thoughts. A military track approached from behind; I did not turn around to see what it was but continued to walk close to the edge of the road. All of a sudden, the vehicle swerved toward me, and the driver sounded his horn clamorously just behind my ears. Taken by surprise, I gave a start and lunged to the very limits of the pavement. It missed me by an inch, and the soldiers laughed vociferously, hugely tickled. Their mirth would probably have been greater if I had made a false movement and been crushed to death by the wheels. Poor fellows! I felt almost like a benefactor for bringing some happiness into the desert of their inane lives!

The Japanese certainly relied far more on brute force than propaganda to conquer and keep populations in subjection—hence their abominable cruelty. Their confidence in their strength also accounted for their deplorable diplomacy and for their initiative in defying the world and the League of Nations, that shimmering fabric of fancies, when they invaded Manchuria in 1931. A country ruled by military leaders expectedly cared less for winning hearts than breaking heads. This is not to say that they had no use for the art of hypocrisy and pretended kindness, but their cultivation of this was insignificant compared to their emphasis on force.

Slavishness toward superiors was inculcated into them as a duty so much so that it had become ingrained. They were as aware of their abject nature as of treading on a hair. Toward their officers, ranging from the highest to the pettiest, they displayed a singular submissiveness, saluting them even when they saw only their backs. After performing this rite many times a day, they probably felt somewhat weary, for I occasionally saw a soldier hiding behind a pillar and pretending not to notice an approaching officer.

The two chief pleasures of the Japanese soldier were drunkenness and debauchery. For months after the occupation, the streets of Hong Kong were still deserted even as early as eight o'clock at night, as much for fear of robbers as for fear of soldiers, who reeled along after imbibing prodigious amounts of sake. It was common to see a petty officer escorted by guards staggering on his way.

The individual soldier was not all brutality. If a person struck up an acquaintance with one of them, he could be quite friendly and considerate. However much a government may attempt to cast its citizens in one mold, they may still differ. Not all soldiers were scoundrels; if they were, the atrocities would have been even more scandalous. Some people told me that their Japanese acquaintances, on finding that they were students whose studies had been interrupted, expressed the hope that they would be able to go to Tokyo soon for their education. There were those who restrained their colleagues from perpetrating foul deeds, as they took no delight in them.

Half a century of uninterrupted triumphs had changed the character of the Japanese military. In the war with Russia they could behave gallantly, probably because they were fighting a Western power for the first time and were testing themselves. After their conquest of Manchuria and after they had shown their defiance of the world by leaving the League of Nations, they had no use for chivalry. When the China War broke out, they showed their rampant character, as evidenced especially in the atrocities they perpetrated on the fall of Nanking. In the Pacific War they cast aside inhibitions of all kinds, and they proclaimed that they were not following any international conventions in their treatment of prisoners of war.

In Hong Kong, horrors were not as monstrous as some enacted in other theaters of war. There was no death march from Bataan when, after the capture of the fortress, the captives (whether they were wounded or not) were made to walk seventy-five miles to prison. Hungry, thirsty, and hot, beaten if they stopped, killed if they could not keep up with the march, about eight thousand persons perished. There was no death railway when, to construct a railway of 250 miles through marsh and jungle from

Thailand to Burma, 46,000 prisoners of war were herded together from Southeast Asia in addition to a horde of coolies. They were treated worse than slaves, and they died like flies in the endeavor to complete the task in a fraction of the time needed.

It is probable that the creed of Bushido, the Japanese ideal of military behavior, of chivalry, was derived from the famous Chinese historical novel, *Romance of the Three Kingdoms*. This lengthy romance, dealing with the attempts of diverse adventurers to snatch the empire on the decay of the Han Dynasty about AD 200, abounds in stories of bravery, loyalty, and self-sacrifice as well as numerous examples of guile and treachery. The Japanese seem to have learned the latter to perfection. In their legends of their victories over the Ainus—the hairy, aboriginal inhabitants of Japan, whom their ancestors exterminated—their heroes were exuberantly lauded for wily exploits employing deceit, which Homer would never have dreamed of attributing to Achilles. Even in their famous story of "The Forty-seven Ronins," whose heroism makes them the wonder of the people, the principal character plotted revenge on his master's murderer and, in order to disarm suspicion, dissimulated his character and lived the life of an apparently useless libertine. It would appear that bravery cannot exist without guile. The modern examples of their deceitfulness are seen in the manufactured incidents that led to the attack on Manchuria in 1931 and the general war in China in 1937, in the sudden onslaughts on Pearl Harbor and other targets while their envoys were engaged in deceptive palaver in Washington, and in their broken promises of honorable treatment for armies that surrendered to them in Singapore and other places.

As they knew that their own trustworthiness was nonexistent, they naturally placed no faith in others. As they never kept their promises, they were vigilantly suspicious of other people's declarations. They used to be forever babbling of China's "insincerity" as an excuse for aggression. Opportunism was the keynote of their policy. They had no ideals, no moral scruples. They were beyond good and evil; Nietzsche had nothing to teach them.

The Japanese military code by which soldiers taken captive were to consider themselves disgraced accounted not only for their bravery but also for their cruelty. They fought to the death or committed suicide rather than surrendering. Such fanaticism might merit praise if it were exercised on behalf of a just cause. If they preferred to blow themselves up with hand grenades rather than become prisoners of war, that was their own business and such action might even win admiration. But the little value they placed on their own lives was outdistanced by the tremendous contempt they felt for the lives of other people. When they had no compunction about indulging in murders—whether of the individual or en masse, whether for sport or in the heat of battle—something must have been very wrong with them.

It would not do to resort to the excuse that war conditions were the cause of their behavior. The simple reason is that they were not forced on them; they had been cherishing the ideal of war and had deliberately engineered the outbreak of hostilities. Furthermore, war conditions applied just as much to the other combatants, who did not behave in the same way. If such conditions could be held accountable for atrocious conduct then, instead of serving as a cover, they should be categorically condemned. Attempts should have been made to see that they did not arise. The Japanese warmongers were therefore responsible for the conditions and the behavior of their troops.

The trouble with the Japanese was that for decades, in their anxiety to imitate the West, they responded most eagerly to its brand of militarism. This might be due to historical causes, but it could also be due to their national character. When they had made themselves into a modern military power, they found that their neighbor, China, was the prey of the Western powers, and so they considered it proper to step in and take part in the same game. With success their appetite grew. They took Germany as a model. However, they displayed their shocking brutalities in China even before the Nazis unleashed their horrors with the outbreak of the Second World War. They were not as bad as the Germans, though, for they had no systematic plan of genocide.

Japan could have won general admiration if it had not become bloated with overweening ideas of its destiny. Considering the small size of its territory and its lack of natural resources, it was extremely surprising that it should have come to play such a major role in world affairs; in the first decades of the twentieth century it was the only Asian country that could stand up to the imperialistic West. But it chose to follow in the footsteps of the most aggressive European countries and outdo them in their contempt for Eastern peoples.

It would be untrue to say that the Japanese are by nature militaristic. No people in history has ever maintained a military tradition forever. In the two centuries between the aggressions of the Portuguese and the fall of the shogunate in 1868, Japan was quite peaceful and was interested only in keeping foreigners out, not in military adventures into other lands. It was

Japan's reaction to Western imperialism that made it blatantly aggressive, but this does not exonerate its imperialism.

The energy of the Japanese could well be praised. It was this that accounted for the successful modernization of their society, but energy, like many other characteristics, could run along wrong as well as right lines. If their prodigious industry had been exclusively applied to making their country great culturally and prosperous economically without affecting other peoples adversely, there could be nothing invidious about it. But when it resulted in restless endeavors to benefit themselves at the expense of their neighbors, it became as praiseworthy as the enterprise of the hawk and the wolf.

It is typical of aggressors that when they receive a dose of the treatment they dish out to others, they scream themselves hoarse at what they term its monstrosity. They do not consider that what they have done to others might be viewed as reprehensible. After the first air raid on Japan, the Japanese were hysterical over the alleged bombing of residential districts, farming villages, hospitals, and schools, with civilians and children as victims; the strikes were regarded as inhuman. Apparently they forgot about their antics over countless cities.

If it had not been for the leaders and schemers subtly imposing the policy of militarism on the people, the ordinary Japanese would not have developed the atrocious behavior they chose to display as conquerors in captured lands. Indoctrinated with a false sense of superiority, they became unbearable. It was not nature that made them ruffians; it was military success, which had gone to the heads of those who had captured the power of the state and who, unable or unwilling to realize their limitations, brought untold misery to others and later to themselves. Those responsible for the transitory victories little realized the fearful retribution they would bring on their people.

I have in the course of these pages given an account of Japanese militarism in those days in order to depict the nature of militarism and foreign aggression. The events are of the past, but there is no reason to presume that militarism, not necessarily Japanese, is dead; wherever and whenever it appears the militarists, human nature being what it is, will behave in much the same way. It is desirable that people should be reminded now and then of this greatest of human pests: militarism, which results in territorial aggression. Things past are not of no account but serve as indicators of future possibilities. History is repetitive of good and bad events alike.

6. Discourses and Conversations

For some time after the fall of Hong Kong, a considerable number of overseas students continued to reside in the university hostels, though some of them lived in the homes of their local friends. Their plight was deplorable, for they had to depend on their slender resources. The main buildings of the university, situated much lower than the hostels, were occupied by a detachment of soldiers, and nobody was allowed to approach their precincts. The students left the university grounds by means of another gate, which emerged on Lyttelton Road.

The existence of the students in the hostels attracted the attention of the Japanese authorities, owing probably to the reports of the officers, who occasionally came to dwell in the houses formerly belonging to members of the academic staff. One day, an officer of the gendarmerie, who was standing on the veranda of a house where an army doctor was temporarily living, noticed four students walking about the grounds. He approached them and asked what they were supposed to be doing. The Japanese were very suspicious of groups of people hobnobbing together. One of them replied that they were trying to keep looters away and, on being asked on whose orders, mentioned that they were acting on instructions from the head of the university. Further questions made the student innocently state that the head was an Englishman, whereupon the officer—who was of an unusual size for a Japanese, being full six feet tall and proportionately stout to boot—went well-nigh berserk and dealt the speaker such a terrific blow on the head that he fell with a crash, bringing down with him his comrades, who were standing at his side. The officer then bellowed that as Hong Kong was now a possession of the Japanese, the university and all that appertained thereto were likewise theirs, and that the students were not to take orders from anybody save the Japanese authorities.

That day he issued a command to the students to send representatives to meet him at his office. None of the students were willing to go but, after a good deal of debate, they came to the conclusion that, if all disregarded the order, the entire body of students might be exterminated, and so a few allowed themselves to be persuaded and went. At the meeting the officer delivered a bombastic speech. He talked of the glory of Japan, the rule of the Europeans over the greater part of Asia, the determination of the Japanese to expel them and keep Asia for the Asians, the similarity of the Japanese and the Chinese in race and culture, the triumph of Japanese arms everywhere, and a lot besides, all to the same effect. Turning from politics to the university, he said that it would be reopened and that the students would have an opportunity to pursue their studies, that he would send them to their homes when communications were restored, and that he would help them as much as possible. The purpose of the meeting was, really, to impress the students with the view that Hong Kong was now solidly under Japanese domination and that they might as well consider themselves Japanese subjects for good. Soon afterward, he ceased to interest himself in the students any further but reported them to the Education Department, whose chief next appeared on the scene.

This gentleman looked more typically like his race, being extremely short and squat. After presenting himself several times to observe the life of the students, he also ordered a delegation to meet him at his office located in a hotel. At the conference it appeared that the person who actually wanted to meet them was a military officer of high rank, who too proceeded to give a speech. It ran along the usual lines, for the Japanese seemed to have certain standard texts in mind. He unfolded more or less the same stuff as the officer of the gendarmerie but went one step further, for he indulged in prophecy that Canada, Australia, and India would very shortly be conquered, according to him, and the outcome of the war would see Europe under the domination of Germany and Asia united under the rule of the Asians. When this stage was reached, the struggle between races would commence. The Europeans headed by the Germans and the Asians under the Japanese would enter on a final, terrific struggle for world supremacy. His vision stopped at this; he did not mention which race would emerge triumphant and whether there would eventually be a war of the worlds between the earth and Mars! Apparently, he had not read H.G. Wells or else his dream would have been more grandiose. But, in an enthusiastic voice he called on all those present to prepare themselves for this glorious, titanic conflict between continents. The students were dismissed to digest the vision as best as they could.

The views of this officer might be taken as representative of those of his nation. Japan and Germany, even while they were ostensibly allies locked in struggle with the rest of the world, were already thinking of the day when they would be at loggerheads with each other. The Axis powers were just like robbers engaged in temporary partnership: the bond was of the weakest and would snap the moment their interests clashed. How else could it be otherwise? The Oriental partner regarded itself as of special descent and the Occidental was entranced with the Nordic myth. Both considered war the *summum bonum*—the greatest good—and would consequently fight until there was no further opportunity for them to do so. The chief of the Education Department came once or twice again but soon ceased his visits and left the students to their fate.

As for the soldiers residing on the university grounds, none were stationed there for long, but batch came to relieve batch. They were rather curious about the students and sometimes trotted up to the hostels. They might enter into conversation with them, the medium of communication being Chinese written characters. It was not always easy to construe their fragments of sentences, and mutual understanding had, in fact, to be eked out by signs. One or two of them could speak broken English and, curiously enough, though the Japanese as a rule condemned the language, those who had just managed to scrape an acquaintance with it displayed their knowledge proudly. I heard one soldier, who had been to school in the United States, lament the fact that few of his compatriots could converse in English, so that since his return to his native land his fluency in it had greatly diminished. Many of the soldiers again had been through campaigns in China and sojourned there several years and could give vent to a few phrases of Mandarin, but most of them seemed not to have been to Canton for any length of time, for it was rare to encounter one who could utter even a single word in Cantonese. From what I could gather here and there, I should like to record some statements of the soldiers as revelations of their character and opinions. I myself sometimes had the opportunity to study them closely and enter into conversation with a soldier now and then. They often talked with surprising frankness, for they in all probability considered the students harmless.

I had the impression that they were war-weary and ardently longed for the day when they could make a sweet return to the land of cherry blossoms. Many of them had seen service in Peiping and Hankow and had been away from home for several years. One stout fellow told me that when he left Osaka his child was two years old; by the time he rejoined his family he would find it difficult to recognize him. They had no great love for the soldier's life. One unusually short chap, full of merriment and devoted to the bottle, stated that he was averse to being a sentry and that nothing was more boring than standing like a statue. Another pointed to an ordinary suit of Western-style clothing and exclaimed that it was fine and attractive and that he felt his uniform was unbecoming. I accidentally came upon two men dressed in tweed suits complete with crimson ties and wearing felt hats waiting to have their photographs taken in the open air. What struck me was their queer appearance, especially when one of them doffed his headgear, revealing a shaven pate. It took me a few moments to realize that they were soldiers who had borrowed their outfit in order that they might have pictures of themselves in glittering, civilian array. As I passed them I must have ill-concealed my surprise, for they suddenly laughed and one in his embarrassment dropped his hat.

But tired as they were of war, it did not mean that the morale of the rank and file was crumbling. The soldiers, whether they liked war or not, would fight doggedly partly from a sense of duty, but mostly from sheer habit of obedience. They were animate robots. How many observers in 1941 fondly imagined that Japan was in no position to embark on further adventures, one of the chief premises usually put forward, being that it was war-weary? Its spurt of spirit astonished everybody.

The soldiers possessed very nebulous ideas about the probable duration of hostilities, though they all admitted that the dawn of real peace would not arise for a very long time to come. One gave his opinion that the war would last another ten years, a conclusion likewise held by most of his comrades. He stated that after the conflict in the East was over there would come the struggle between Asia and Europe. Apparently, all ranks of the army believed in the ultimate emergence of the great racial war.

Those who came to the university were veterans—mostly between twenty-five and thirty years old. According to their own statements few were married. They seemed to yearn to settle down to family life and to be sick of the perpetual transfer from one strange locality to another. It would appear that, as farmers and tailors, as ordinary citizens and neighbors, they would not have been obnoxious at all. But as soldiers, actuated by a sense of false patriotism, they were intolerable.

The soldiers in the university area did not display the ferocity we had come to associate with those in the streets. They seemed to be different people, but of course they were the same persons, who in other circumstances would not hesitate to maltreat or murder their foes or victims. They were just showing another aspect of their character. It is not at all odd for a person to combine kindness and cruelty. He might behave differently to different people at different times; he may be good under one set of circumstances and bad under another. When we attribute a specific trait to a certain individual, what it actually means is that he generally behaves in that way or that he behaves in that way to us. We, however, have the tendency to fancy that a man never deviates from the picture we have built up of him and feel surprised when he does.

The Japanese, before their military fangs were displayed all too flagrantly, were praised for their politeness, and foreigners were thrilled and charmed to see them bowing to the ground so beautifully. They might still possess this empty, ritualistic behavior among their own people, but it was not in evidence in the streets of Hong Kong. However, the soldiers on the university grounds were not rude. Once to my surprise a soldier, who was just five feet tall and whom I knew slightly, came to my room at the hostel. I was then trying to learn the Japanese language and, seeing my book, he was hugely pleased. We discoursed with difficulty on various things but not the war, and on his departure he made a traditional bow, the first and only one I ever received from a Japanese at that time.

I sometimes wondered what made the soldiers tick and bang. Were they naturally brave, diligent, devoted to their country and their emperor, ready to die fighting, contemptuous of other peoples, especially the Chinese, ready to torture and kill those whom they vanquished? Were they fanatics who never reasoned against their superiors, automatons thoroughly controlled by discipline? There were the kamikaze pilots who flew to certain death in running their planes against ships, soldiers who preferred to die rather than surrender, and wounded men who shot at their enemies while these were endeavoring to rescue them after the battle was over. Or were they ordinary, peaceable citizens, given to Buddhism and art and the tea ceremony, brimming with courtesy? Quite possibly when they were in uniform they behaved in one way and when they were out of it they conducted themselves in another.

The Japanese were normally of a suspicious turn of mind, and it was fairly odd that they did not seem to suspect the students of any clandestine activities. It was true that the students had none. Unlike their counterparts in the universities of China who were highly conscious politically and who were perpetually engaged in agitation—now against their government, now against the Japanese, now against the Westerners—the students of Hong Kong University had never in prewar days entertained any interest in politics. Their horizon was limited to their academic studies and play. In fact, they were model students, perfectly harmless. Possibly the Japanese were aware of this, and it accounted for their comparative friendliness, judging from the way they behaved in China. They did nothing for the students—it would have been quite out of character for them to do so—but they did not molest them.

It would be fanciful to suppose that the academic nature of the place influenced the behavior of the soldiers! And yet one is tempted to make the supposition. I do not recall that any violent incident ever occurred on the grounds of the university. The European members of the academic staff were among the last to go to the internment camp at Stanley. In the meantime, they were allowed to occupy their former quarters, and I never heard that any of them suffered any atrocity at the hands of the Japanese.

Both officers and men, generally speaking, became gentler in the university precincts. They could even be considerate, and there was an occasional instance of helpfulness. I had an acquaintance who was Vietnamese, an arts student. He came to know a Japanese officer who was working in the university library for a few days selecting books for shipment to Japan. This officer possessed some knowledge of French, and he was delighted to converse in that language with the Vietnamese with whom it was his medium of education in school. The Vietnamese was anxious to return to his native land, and he asked the officer for help. The officer, it so happened, was going to French Indo-China within a short time and, to the delight of the stranded student, he took him along with him on the pretext that he needed a French-speaking secretary.

It was not uncommon to see Japanese soldiers, when off duty though still in uniform, wandering around the hostels and greeting students smilingly to show their friendliness. During such times they did not appear to be the ferocious, fanatical fighters they were reported to be. Naturally, the students were wary of them, for they knew well enough that their horrible reputations were not without foundation. But looking at them with their amiable manners and pleasant talk, one could hardly believe that in other circumstances they were ready to commit the most frightful deeds.

As each of the students managed to scrape together by some means or other enough for traveling expenses and, in accordance with what he considered the appropriate time, he left Hong Kong. The students entered China in diverse groups and by different routes. Most of them resumed their studies at various Chinese universities.

I should like to record a rather amusing incident that befell a student. He was engaged in packing his luggage when a soldier, who had spoken with him once or twice before, chanced to drop in and, on perceiving him thus occupied, inquired where he was removing. The student, who was noted for his jocose temperament and oftentimes gave utterance to words that were rather out of harmony with the time and place, blurted out with energy that he was leaving for Chungking, whereupon the soldier vanished like a bolt. He was left to regret his rash indiscretion, with forebodings of a firing squad returning and shooting him dead on the spot for his untimely confession. After the lapse of about twenty minutes, however, the same soldier came back with half a dozen tins of corned beef, which he had fetched from his store, and presented them to him with his compliments, requesting him to eat them on his journey. Apparently, he had no antipathy toward Chungking.

7. Later Events

As the months rolled away, Hong Kong assumed a less military aspect and conditions appeared to be a bit more normal. Fewer soldiers were seen in the streets, the majority having seemingly been whisked away to perish gloriously in other, more active theaters of combat. A few trams and buses ran and shops reopened, displaying but attenuated stocks of goods. Though the town was electrically lit at night, the shops closed early and few pedestrians trod the pavements, as safety was an ever-present consideration by virtue of its absence. Turmoil and excitement had abated to a large extent; groaning quiet pervaded the atmosphere—the quiet of death.

The cost of living resembled steam in that it inexorably rose upward. Rice became a government monopoly and each person was allowed to purchase only 6.4 tahils a day, barely enough for two miserable bowls, with the consequence that anemia and emaciation increased at an alarming rate. The government attempted to control and ration other foodstuffs, such as flour, sugar, and oil, but they were distributed in meager quantities. The purchaser, who had few if any enjoyments, was given the pleasure of cooling his heels for a whole day in a long queue to obtain them. Starvation did not cease to take its diurnal toll of lives, and the streets exhibited almost as ghastly a spectacle as ever.

Prices of most commodities, immediately after the occupation, soared to four times their prewar level; some, such as tobacco, even higher. But they now became prohibitive. What with business unable to struggle out of the gloomy pool of stagnancy, even the merchants found it difficult to live.

To make matters worse, the government in its wisdom, without any previous announcement, suddenly in July further depreciated the value of the Hong Kong currency, four dollars being now equivalent to one military yen. One phenomenon revealed the mind of the populace. Many were in the habit of accumulating the notes in use in the colony before the crash, as they had unbounded confidence in its recapture by the British; even now, though they had to sustain heavy losses owing to their unexpected depreciation, they still continued to hoard them so that these notes became scarce. A black market somersaulted into existence, in which a ten-yen note could be exchanged for only thirty Hong Kong dollars.

To prevent an epidemic of cholera that was endemic in Hong Kong from breaking out, the authorities instituted compulsory inoculations of the people en masse at periodical intervals. An inoculation service was formed. Squads were sent around the territory to do the work; they went from house to house systematically and also stationed themselves in streets to stop passersby. Each inoculated person was given a certificate, which was a small sheet of red paper. At first, a squad consisted of four persons accompanied by two soldiers. Later, the soldiers disappeared and their places were taken by Formosan nurses. Later again, the nurses vanished. There was nothing particularly objectionable about the anticholera campaign save that it was not really necessary and the compulsory exercise was annoying to many people. The soldiers slapped those who raised the slightest objection to the treatment, and the inoculations were not always performed with gentleness, this depending on the whims of the inoculators who were generally unqualified for the work.

Toward the end of February, a celebration was staged to rejoice over the fall of Singapore, and the Council of Representatives received orders to hold a procession. Unluckily, the day turned out to be inauspicious, for it drizzled and the roads were muddy. Before the procession started in Statue Square, the chief of the representatives shouted, "Banzai," to be unenthusiastically reverberated by the participants. What a contrast between the usual Chinese procession, with its spontaneous joy, and that dismal specimen! Most of the ingredients were there, the color and the music, but the spirit was absent. The paper flags, centrally painted with the red disk of the rising sun, seemed to be held in nerveless hands, ready to drop them. The procession wended its way through the main streets up toward Wanchai then to the Western Market. Spectators in doorways and windows looked on with lackluster eyes. There were no crowds to surge forward, entranced. Hardly a sound, not a cheer rent the air, save from the Japanese soldiers and civilians, who stood in groups outside their offices and residences, waving their flags. Well might the populace look dispirited, for two months of misrule had convinced them of the tyranny of the new government, of the hopeless outlook for the future, of nothing but adversity in the Co-Prosperity Sphere. What cause for jubilation was there that one more city should succumb to their aggressive arms?

After all, were not the majority of the inhabitants of Singapore Chinese, and would they not suffer as much or even more than their brethren in Hong Kong? When Singapore was undergoing assaults more terrible than those of Hong Kong, the newspapers painted with horrid glee lurid pictures of its rapid reduction to ruins. It was described as a flaming inferno with the Japanese troops and planes scattering destruction from left and right. After its fall, they announced with unconcealed delight that seventy thousand Chinese had been arrested on that island, the release of this bit of news being apparently intended to strike terror into the hearts of the Hong Kong populace. Asinine indeed were the Japanese authorities, for did not this prove all too clearly that, wherever their forces went, the Chinese were their chief targets of attack, the principal sufferers? Not only in China but elsewhere in countries belonging to other governments this was the case, and yet they impertinently babbled of the special ties between the two races. Singapore became Shonan; little news appeared in Hong Kong after its capture, but one could well envisage its condition.

Vast numbers of people continued to quit Hong Kong. It was not easy indeed for many to do so, for their families had resided there for generations and they had their roots there. In the natural world, every material body is endowed with inertia, it having a tendency to remain where it is unless some force is potent enough to shift it from its position. So is it with the human mind whose property of inertia, called habit, is just as strong. Every man moves along accustomed grooves, and it requires a tremendous effort to tear him away from what is familiar. Lucky is he when the incentive comes in the form of a happy event, but more often it is tragedy that is most effective. Such a mass migration, as I saw unrolled before my eyes, was an affair that I never thought would ever be mine to witness. But then there are many events, momentous and trivial, that come to pass without their ever having entered one's dreams before.

Hong Kong constituted only a comparatively insignificant part of the arena of the Pacific War. On the day that Japan initiated hostilities, it bombed not only Hong Kong but Pearl Harbor, Manila, Guam, Singora, and Singapore as well. Thailand succumbed speedily without a fight. Hong Kong fell quite early owing to its small extent of territory and its proximity to China, where Japan had large armies.

It is strange that—though the Americans and the British were having strained relations with the Japanese, there was tension in the air for some time, and imminent hostilities were probable—the sudden onslaughts of the enemy took them by surprise, and their preparations everywhere for the conflict were inadequate. The United States Pacific fleet at Pearl Harbor was at ease, quite unsuspicious of what was about to happen. The Japanese bombers and fighters had a field day; in one and a half hours they had wiped out a great fleet at the cost of less than thirty planes. Just as amazing was the sinking in the South China Sea of the new giant British battleships, the Prince of Wales and the Repulse, by eighty-five torpedo bombers and high-level bombers off the east coast of Malaya; the warships were not provided with air cover.

After bombing Singapore, the enemy did not attempt to capture it straightway but invaded Malaya from Thailand and by landing in Kota Bahru from ships, which had sailed from Hainan Island captured from China in 1939, and proceeded to move southward. By the time that Hong Kong fell, they had taken Penang and were somewhere near Ipoh. Their shock troops, hardened in the China theater, besieged Singapore then crossed the Johore Strait in landing craft and collapsible rafts and streamed ashore on the northwest part of the island. They obtained its surrender on February 15. Singapore was a more important naval base than Hong Kong and was regarded as an impregnable fortress. Plans for defense of the island were based on the assumption that assaults would be made by sea on its south side where the city was located. Hardly anything was prepared to counter a land attack from Johore. The British argued that it would be impracticable for the Japanese to traverse the length of the Malay Peninsula and that, if they were rash enough to do such a thing, their progress could easily be checked before they reached the island.

Comparing the Battle of Singapore with the Battle of Hong Kong, we find that the former lasted fifteen days—that is, for about the same period of time as the latter, which occupied fourteen days. Singapore was separated from Johore by a strait, while between Hong Kong and Kowloon was a harbor. In both cases, the British were pitted against the Japanese, and they could see one another across the narrow stretches of water. In Hong Kong, however, it was the city that faced the mainland, whereas in Singapore, the city was on the far side of the island. Singapore turned out to be as ill defended as Hong Kong—enemy aircraft flew over the island to unload their bombs unopposed. In either case, it took a week from the time the enemy effected a landing on the island for it to surrender.

After the fall of Singapore, the Japanese turned their attention to the Dutch East Indies, which were under the rule of a governor and which were cut off from the colonizing country now occupied by the Nazis. They dispatched a big invasion fleet, which on February 27 fell in with an Allied fleet under the command of a Dutch admiral and which totally defeated it in the Battle of the Java Sea. The Japanese aircraft had a clear field, for the Dutch had no planes to fight them. Japanese troops soon occupied the huge East Indian archipelago, a fertile source of raw materials, including oil.

The Japanese invaders entered Burma from Thailand and captured Rangoon in early March. Their advance was more difficult thereafter, and Mandalay did not fall until May 6. They stopped at Assam Preparatory to launch an invasion against India. With the loss of Burma, land communication between Chungking and the outside world slithered from the precarious to nil.

The conquest of the Philippines proceeded smoothly in the initial stages. The Japanese landed troops easily, as the American fleet was too small to make any effective opposition and, within a few weeks, had overrun the archipelago, Manila falling on January 2, 1942. However, the Americans and Filipinos, who were forced to retreat to Bataan and Corregidor, were able to hold out for some months before surrendering to fierce attacks of shock troops dispatched from Singapore.

Later the Japanese managed to wrest a few islands strewn over the Pacific, including the Aleutians, New Guinea, and the Solomons. Within a few strange months, they had subdued the whole of Southeast Asia and had become lords of the western Pacific Ocean. They had defeated the mighty democracies of the United States and Great Britain. They were poised for conquests further afield of India and Australia. They had reason to feel vastly elated, and victory after victory not only delighted the ears of those in their homeland but was trumpeted without delay through the radio and the press in Hong Kong.

But hot on the heels of their series of victories came reverses, which signaled the end of their triumphs and loomed as portents of dark days ahead. However, the defeats were not admitted publicly.

In May, a Japanese task force set out to capture Port Moresby in Australian New Guinea. Battle was waged in the Coral Sea where the Japanese lost one carrier and had another badly damaged, while on the Allied side, likewise one carrier was sunk and another hit. The battle was a draw, but the Japanese regarded it as a great victory. Actually, it was damaging to them, for not only had they failed in their aim of taking Port Moresby, but they had lost many experienced naval pilots whom they found almost impossible to replace.

Then again the Japanese sent a strong fleet to conquer the Midway Atoll, which was on the route to Hawaii. Battle was joined in early June with the Japanese starting off by bombing the island. The Americans were at first unsuccessful in their attempts to bomb the Japanese aircraft carriers, but later their dive-bombers swooped down from a high altitude and wrecked all the four Japanese carriers, which burned away and sank into the deep. The Japanese planes, having no carriers on which to land, found their grave in the ocean, as they exhausted their fuel supply. The attacking navy was forced to withdraw, with U.S. planes and submarines chasing after and further damaging it. Though fought at sea, this was in actuality an air battle, for the battleships, destroyers, and cruisers took no real part. The Japanese attempted to twist the facts of this colossal disaster and gave out all sorts of fantastic reasons to refute the American claims. Thus they kept up their morale and deceived the conquered peoples to whom truth was an invisible star innumerable light-years away.

Later in New Guinea and the Solomon Islands, the Japanese likewise had to listen to the grievous music of defeat. Failing to capture Fort Moresby by sea, they endeavored to take it by land but met with no better success. A force of 15,000 men proceeding from Buna in the northwest part of New Guinea was halted just a few miles from its objective and was ingloriously driven back to the beach of the place from which it started, and what remained of it was annihilated. In nearby Solomon Islands, American marines proceeding from New Zealand and taking the offensive captured Guadalcanal, and they could not be dislodged in the ensuing bitter fights. In the naval conflicts in the area, which lasted for months, the Japanese, who were trying to relieve their land forces, were finally decisively defeated.

After the fall of Mandalay, the rugged Burma Road to China was closed. For a short time it looked as though Mandalay would be strangled for lack of supplies. However, to the surprise of everyone, this predicament was resolved when the United States organized an air ferry over "the hump" of the formidable Himalaya Mountains. The Japanese stated that they were launching an attack from North Burma and, for a few days, they would report their penetration deeper into Yunnan when, suddenly, all news of that arena ceased. They were forever predicting the collapse of the Chungking regime and described with gusto the difficulties, partially imaginary, in which it was enmeshed.

The first air raid that Japan had ever sustained in its history occurred on April 18, 1942. For long it had enjoyed the glory of unleashing bombs over China and recently over other countries. It had come to believe it was immune to air attack. Now, out of a clear sky in broad daylight, sixteen U.S. bombers made a raid extending over a few hours. The planes were launched from a carrier, but they flew to land in China. The majority of the men parachuted into occupied China but were helped by friendly Chinese to get to Free China, and only eight of the fliers were captured by the enemy. The Japanese foamed with consternation, dread, and fury. No news of the attack was released in Hong Kong, as it would have had a bad effect on the spirits of the conquered people.

8. Departure

Sometime after the fall of Hong Kong, I made up my mind to quit it. But I lingered on for a few months longer because I was impelled by curiosity to observe the workings of the Co-Prosperity Sphere and to find out whether there was any truth in the claims of the conquerors. I had heard and read so much about the Japanese and their aggressions in China, but I had never seen how they administered captured territory. I did not wish to think ill of them from mere prejudice, to be irrationally antagonistic toward them; I tried to keep an open mind, to evaluate them with dispassionate interest. If I henceforth became opposed to them, I had good reasons for so doing. Another cause of my holding on was the hope that I might get some news of my family in Malaya. After it was quite clear that I could not communicate with my people and when I had nothing more that I wanted to learn about the aggressors, I left Hong Kong.

I had been making the required preparations for some time. There was no necessity for me to rush into China in panic. I had to find out the most convenient route to take and to go along with people who were more familiar with the conditions. My friends and I spent a lot of time discussing our plans. I bought a black suit of the clothing worn by Chinese peasants consisting of a loose coat and trousers, changed my Hong Kong dollars into Chinese national currency, and put all my goods into a leather bag and a capacious canvas sack.

Our party of twenty-four persons comprised ten university students and a merchant with his family. I was not previously acquainted with the merchant, who was to lead the way and to whom I was then introduced by a friend. On the evening of July 30, 1942, we left Hong Kong Island and went over to Kowloon to pass the night in his house in Shum Shui

Po. It was one of a row of three-story brick houses, but we were cramped for space, as he occupied only the first floor and there were so many of us. We went to bed early.

The next morning we woke up betimes and had a breakfast of congee. By eight o'clock all our luggage was packed into a truck, which was filled almost to its full capacity, leaving a narrow space at the back where some of us could stand, the remainder of the passengers sitting on top of the luggage. It was a moot point who were the more uncomfortable—those who sat or those who stood. I had never traveled in a truck in this manner before, but later I was to experience even worse conditions. The vehicle started, and shortly thereafter rain fell in mild streams wetting us as it lumbered along. We entered the New Territories, formerly so beloved of tourists; even now the countryside smiled entrancingly enough, but it was with an ineffable air of weariness, of disillusionment, of tragedy that had swept over it. With what plaintive beauty gleamed the sea and how majestically sorrowful looked the mountains opposite as we jogged along after passing Taipo!

As we came across sentry posts at five different places along the route, our truck had to stop for a longer or shorter period, depending on the whims of the soldiers. All of us clambered down, and the vehicle was searched. We were considered to be in luck, for the gentlemen with bayonets did not care to bother us much, probably on account of the rain; very often, we were told, they would order every piece of luggage to be taken down and its contents littered on the ground. When a truck might contain as many as fifty bags of various descriptions and different sizes, it could well be imagined how much time would be consumed at these stoppages. At a spot five miles from our destination, a bridge had broken down and was not yet repaired. The truck could not proceed any farther, and we had to perform the remainder of our journey on foot. We forded the stream with the water almost up to our waists while a score of porters carried the luggage. The rain continued to fall as we trudged along, a mirthless band. By the time we reached Shataukok, our destination for the day, the shadows of evening had begun to envelop the skies. It had taken us a whole day to make a journey, which not so long ago would have required but a fraction of the time. But our trials for that day were not yet over. At the entrance to the village, Indian policemen under the supervision of a Japanese soldier minutely examined our baggage. The policemen, whose interest in the investigation was stimulated by the possibility of loot, appropriated unto themselves a few articles, such as tins of condensed milk.

One of these wretched policemen, whose subservience to their Japanese masters was a sight to behold, apparently tried to be facetious and asked a friend of mine, who had a good quantity of toilet articles, like soap, shaving cream, and toothpaste in his bag, whether he was a barber. The Japanese soldier did not utter a word or take anything but looked with keen interest at the proceedings, his rifle slung behind his back. When the lengthy inspection was at last over, we entered the village and, after inquiries, found a dilapidated inn in which to pass the night.

Shataukok, situated beside Mirs Bay on the northeastern part of the New Territories, was a small fishing village of Hakkas. Located on the boundary of the colony, it was of a straggling character, quite dirty, and not more picturesque than any other village. The prices of goods were higher than in the city and were quoted in terms of Chinese national currency. The inhabitants were a stolid lot, and their lives could not have been easy even in peaceful times. We took our dinner at a roadside stall. My friends and I then wandered around the place for a while by way of a superfluous constitutional before returning to the inn. There was nothing to detain us in that village, and we were only anxious to leave it as soon as possible, away from this last bit of Japanese-occupied territory. Our spirits mounted at the prospect. We made our beds on the creaky, wooden floor, which could have been considerably cleaner. We all stayed in one large hall, and all the light we enjoyed came from a single oil lamp. As we lay down to rest, we thought of the morrow when we would be quit of those who had disrupted our lives.

When the morning broke, a wind blew lightly and the skies looked overcast. We rose, and at nine o'clock we gathered at a pier a few hundred yards from our inn. What a gloomy scene confronted us, the bleak pier jutting out into the sea, with a number of dirty junks clinging to its sides! Now came what we envisaged was the last ordeal of our departure. At the head of the pier stood a Japanese sentry, who examined our persons and bags with more care than we had encountered at other posts, displaying a rapacity not so shamelessly in evidence in town. He took whatever captured his fancy, and his fancy was of generous proportions. We each lost something, but the worst hit was one of my friends, from whose bags were taken three new shirts, a blanket recently bought, a tin of Quaker Oats, an alarm clock, a torch, and a penknife. One of the merchant's relatives in our party—seeing the soldier seize a valuable fountain pen of his and finger it, open its cap, and scrutinize it with evident interest—grew apprehensive. When the soldier proceeded to deposit it on a stand nearby, he moved forward to snatch it back. The soldier gave him a shove, and he nearly fell off the pier. The merchant told him to keep quiet, and nothing further happened. After collecting a handsome pile at his side, the sentry let us pass. We walked dejectedly to the end of the pier.

We hired two junks and sat down to enjoy the voyage as best we could after all our luggage was stowed on board. As we started, rain fell, and before we had sailed half a mile it dashed down in torrents. Without any awning overhead, we had our clothing completely soaked through. A violent wind blew, bending the boat to one side, and it angrily beat the sea into waves that rocked and crashed around us. As we continued to press forward, our boat nearly capsized; the boatmen considered it inadvisable to proceed further, and there was no alternative for us but to turn back. In what pitiable plight we were as we ascended the very landing that we left two hours ago, never imagining that we would have to return! We were as miserable as chickens rescued from a pond. We walked back in our bedraggled state to the inn, where we cursed our luck and for that day sat disconsolately.

"Our leaving Hong Kong does not seem such a good idea," grumbled Saw Tek Chin, a medical student. He had not been enthusiastic about going to China and had only joined us partly on account of my persuasions.

"Feeling disheartened because of some slight distress?" I asked bravely, as though our plight was an everyday affair. "It is nothing. I enjoy the experience."

"You enjoy the experience!" retorted Tek Chin. "You have a queer sense of enjoyment."

"Life is experience," I said reflectively. "Whether an experience is good or bad, happy or miserable, it is not amiss to have it. It enriches one's life."

"Although I am all for going away from Hong Kong," chimed in Ang Chuan Bee, an engineering student, "I must confess that I never thought we would have so much trouble. I hope that we can be off tomorrow and that we don't meet with any unpleasant occurrences. I feel sore at the soldier taking so many of my things."

"The interior of China is very short of goods," remarked the merchant, whose name was Fou Lok Meng. "They are very costly and, if we don't take in what we need, we'll be unable to afford them."

"That's why I bought as many things as I could afford," said Chuan Bee. He looked glum at his losses.

"I was shocked to see the Jap take my fountain pen," said the relative of the merchant who had tried to retrieve his article. "I had intended to sell it."

"It's better to lose your pen than your life," said the merchant. "You could have concealed it better."

"I knew they liked pens," said the relative. "In the early days of the occupation, the soldiers used to seize them indiscriminately. But latterly seizure of articles has stopped—or so I thought."

"Evidently, it still goes on in out-of-the-way villages," said Chuan Bee. "I did not know we had to be checked at so many points. Luckily, the other soldiers did not take my things. If everyone took as much as this last one, I shall arrive in China with hardly anything."

"I lost little," said Tek Chin, "but our miserable journey hitherto may be just a prelude to something worse." He was thoroughly pessimistic.

"I do not care even if I arrive in China with nothing," declared Lim Seh Huck, an arts student. "And I do not bother about any suffering. All I want is to be away from the Japs."

"You dislike them?" I asked mildly.

"I loathe them," was the violent reply.

"Why?" asked Tek Chin, who had no particular dislike of the Japs. "Have you been ill-treated by them?"

"Once, as I was passing a police station, an officer ordered my arrest and for three hours I had to sit on its dirty floor before I was released. Up to now, I can't understand what my crime was. Another time I was knocked down by a soldier for unwittingly passing a barricade in the street. However, these incidents don't suffice to make me hate them. I think there is something very wrong with them."

"Why didn't you leave Hong Kong earlier?" asked Tek Chin.

"I don't quite understand why either," said Seh Huck musingly. "I suppose that I am a slow mover and it took me some time to make up my mind. I had never thought of going to China in our university days, and it is a strange country to me."

"Your mind is now made up?" questioned Tek Chin inquisitively. "You won't regret going?"

"Never will I regret it," was the emphatic reply. "You are not a resident of Hong Kong, I believe," said the merchant after a short pause. "Where is your home?"

"Singapore," replied Seh Huck.

"Singapore!" exclaimed the merchant. "That's interesting. It's a long way off and you won't be able to go back at present. According to the newspapers, Singapore was even more battered than Hong Kong when it fell. What a pity."

"I am afraid so," said Seh Huck gloomily. "I don't know what kind of a hell the Singaporeans are living in now."

"And they have no place to escape to," chimed in Chuan Bee. "We may consider ourselves a bit luckier."

"I suppose there'll be no trouble in our getting away tomorrow," said Tek Chin.

"There should be none," said the merchant. "The weather is likely to clear up."

"How do you know?" asked Tek Chin morosely.

"I hope we are not caught in an even worse storm. I don't like to be drowned."

I managed a smile. "I don't think any of us likes that," I said soothingly. "If the weather is dangerous, we just stay here."

"What a sorry place to be cooped up in," said Tek Chin unhappily.

"In the interior of China it will be worse," said the merchant.

"Is that so?" exclaimed Tek Chin, consternation showing all over him.

"It might be better for you to return to Hong Kong. It's not too late," said Seh Huck.

"Oh, never mind," said Tek Chin shamefacedly. "If another person can bear it, I suppose I can too."

The rain fell off and on the whole evening and through the night, but the wind gradually abated toward sundown.

An unfortunate incident occurred. Toward the evening, owing to the report of a spy, soldiers raided the boats where our luggage was still stored in the holds in the care of the boatmen, as it would have been inconvenient to have them removed to our inn. They found two hundred watches secreted in a box that, unknown to us, the merchant was trying to smuggle out of Hong Kong. That night at half past eight we were roused from our beds, where we had retired early, by the arrival of soldiers, who examined our persons and peered into every nook and corner of the floor we occupied. After that they did not disturb us any further. It was a moot point what the outcome might be if they reported to their officers, but their avaricious nature caused them to refrain from so doing; they were satisfied with appropriating unto themselves the entire collection of watches!

56

For a long time after the departure of the soldiers, the merchant sat with his family in his part of the apartment lamenting his loss. My friends and I were in another part, and we conversed in a low tone about the incident.

"Imagine such an occurrence," said Tek Chin angrily. "We might all have been sentenced to be shot."

"These merchants are the limit," said Chuan Bee. "However, I suppose smuggling is by no means uncommon."

"He has no right to involve us," said a student who was a quiet person and seldom spoke.

"I don't think he wanted to involve us," I said, "but of course he was only considering his own interests."

The next morning when we awoke, the weather was still none of the best, but we set sail again at eleven o'clock, fervently hoping that we would not have to be driven back a second time. After we had traversed half our journey, the skies cleared and the sun radiated welcome warmth. What beautiful views greeted our eyes! Hills reared themselves in the distance, rising sharply from the coast, and islets studded the sea.

In the evening we reached our destination. The boats had to stop a short distance away from the land, and we waded through the water. We found ourselves on a desolate beach strewn with gray rocks, but this was Free China. While I reclined on the sand, wet and hungry, I felt elated at the reflection that I would have the opportunity to see the country. A li away was the village of Siu Mui Sha and, as we trotted there to pass the night, walking gingerly along narrow, muddy paths across green rice fields, an immense wave of joy swept through me.

9. Kukong

China is a country that automatically conjures up a vision of extensive territories, teeming millions of people, and a history longer in its continuity than any other, stretching from before Greece and Rome to the present day. The sheer extent in terms of both geography and history has been a subject of wonder to other peoples. In the twentieth century, its geographical area did not seem so impressive, there being other states controlling landmasses almost as big or even bigger. But its population has never been surpassed. To European writers, it has even appeared to be in the nature of a continent. Its size and population are comparable to those of Europe. With its many countries, it is deemed a continent but, strictly speaking, it is geographically the western end of the land mass of which China is the eastern end.

Historically, China began in the north in the region of the Hwang Ho, and thence it spread southward and westward. Its direct contact with the outside world was for the greater part of its history almost entirely confined to the various barbarian tribes on its northern, western, and southern flanks. On its eastern side, it is bounded by the vast Pacific Ocean, and in the days of boats and sailing ships cruising along, this ocean was an extremely hazardous enterprise. The Chinese did not take to the sea, and it was the European peoples commencing with the Portuguese in the sixteenth century who first came to China across the waters.

The coastal regions and the plains washed by the three great rivers of the Hwang Ho, Yangtze Kiang, and Si Kiang are thickly bestrewn with cities, having naturally been the easiest to develop. The interior, consisting of vast plateaus and lofty mountains, sparsely populated, had been largely neglected until the loss of the eastern areas to Japan entailed a precipitate migration, which acted like a ferment and caused it to hum with activity. It could not reasonably be expected that a few years resounding with the clangor of feverish war could transform and improve it to any profound extent; although less steeped in somnolence, it was far from modernization. This was the region known as Free China, of which the capital was Chungking, and the government was constituted by the Kuomintang under Generalissimo Chiang Kai-shek. It was to Free China that those Chinese who did not wish to live under Japanese suzerainty fled, and it was to Free China that the inhabitants of the fallen colony of Hong Kong now directed their steps with alacrity. The refugees from many areas spread all over the place. Some might settle down in places not far from their former homes while others might have trekked deep into the interior. Some might have fled helter-skelter before the advancing Japanese troops while others might have gone in later. Some left their homes alone and others came in families. They all knew that the inland areas were not well developed and that they were not going to a life of ease but hardship. But whoever they were—soldier or student, peasant or scholar, coolie or merchant—they left their homes to avoid living under a hated government of swashbucklers. The cost of transport and travel was excessive, and by the time they reached their journey's end, many of these people had practically exhausted their funds. But, funds or no funds, the refugees had to begin life anew. This kind of mass upheaval helped to eradicate parochialism, and many dialects could be heard in a town, a phenomenon unknown before. It wakened the backward hinterland from its medieval slumber and accustomed it to new values and strange ideas, customs, and ways of life.

Siu Mui Sha, where I slept on the first night of my escape to China, was a small village of mud huts and some brick houses. The narrow earth lanes were certainly far from clean. It was typical of its kind, and there was nothing to admire in it. The conditions were primitive—oil lamps and wells supplied light and water, respectively. Presumably the villagers did not depart much from their ancestors' way of life. Pigs and fowl dwelt side by side with human beings, who seemed to care nothing at all for cleanliness. Country air is supposed to be much fresher than the polluted atmosphere of cities, but in this kind of village the air had its own defilement, and its smell was the antithesis of fragrant.

We turned in as soon as it was dark, for light was precious. I lodged in a mud hut. My pallet was of straw spread on a wooden framework, which went by the courteous name of bed. I lay in the dark unable to sleep for some hours. What thoughts floated through my mind! One idea came uppermost—I was now rid of the Japanese and their Co-Prosperity Sphere. I might be living in the Adversity Sphere, but it was preferable. The weather was hot and I felt oppressed—but the oppression was that of the heat, far less intolerable than that exerted by man. I listened to the shrill music of the cicadas in the fields and felt the ecstasy of their freedom. Gradually I dropped off to sleep.

It was still dark when we all awoke and prepared to travel inland. We gathered our belongings and set off on our journey at five o'clock in the morning after a breakfast of congee. Our destination for the day was another village called Pengshan. There were no vehicles of any kind, and we had to walk all the way along a rough and tortuous path, which wound along the rice fields and up and down hills. It drizzled now and then, but we ignored it. When we came to a stream, we forded it. We had porters from the village to carry our heavier luggage, each piece slung at one end of a shoulder-pole, and a guide to lead the way. As we trudged along, we kept up our spirits by desultory converse. We thought of our journey's end and not of our present discomfort. It was the season of longans, and we came across occasional vendors at wayside stalls where we rested and ate this delicious fruit.

As evening drew to a close we reached Pengshan, a village larger than the one we had left that morning. As our clothing and baggage had been soaked in the rain and we were feeling tired and depressed, we decided to spend not only the night but the whole of the next day in this place to dry our things and recuperate our energies. Our party, which comprised not only men but women and children, certainly did not look sprightly after a whole day's tramp. We lodged with the farmers in their huts, and I spent the day chatting with my friends or wandering in the fields where the rice stalks gleamed and the scene was refreshing.

Departing from Pengshan at 7:00 AM, we trekked along a narrow road. The day was sunny and our walk was comparatively pleasant and less fatiguing than before. Along the public road were posts at frequent intervals, each consisting of a flag stuck on a mound, beside which stood the guerillas, who had set them up and who would come down to demand "tea money" from wayfarers. They wore no uniforms, but they carried guns and had cartridge belts. They did not look ferocious and appeared to be in good physical shape. At about 5:00 PM we reached Tamshui, a town of some size. Crowds thronged the streets of cobblestones, and many matsheds had been put up, serving as dwelling places, shops, and restaurants.

The next day we continued our journey, but we no longer had to tax the strength of our patient feet. We took a junk that sailed up the East River or Tung Kiang past pine-covered hills beneath a bright blue sky. We came to the city of Waichow where we passed two nights. I stood on the banks of the river watching the green willows drooping over the waters. I saw enemy planes fly over, and there was an air-raid alarm but they dropped no bombs. After only a few days, I had almost forgotten the existence of the Japanese, but this incident recalled to me that I had entered a country at war.

We took our departure from Waichow at 9:00 PM in a motorboat, which might conceivably hold ten persons in comfort but now had the misfortune to be packed with seventy. It was not possible to lie down at full length although we had to sleep there. The stifling heat was such that sweat poured from us. We lumbered along the brown ripples of the river past villages and bamboo groves. The rickety motor stopped functioning every few hours, but nobody showed any impatience. Sometimes it rained, and then we felt refreshed but uncomfortable too, as we could not avoid getting wet. We spent three days in that awful vessel, but as everything, luckily in cases like ours, must come to an end, we eventually reached our destination for that stage of the journey, a town called Loulong.

This place was smaller than Waichow and appeared medieval in its condition. Its main street was paved with a flat mass of granite blocks, and wheelbarrows were the only vehicles. It was somnolent and was apparently little affected by the war. Most members of our party had fallen ill what with fatigue, heat, rain, and the unsanitary conditions. We stayed in Loulong for five days, trying to find a truck to convey us on the next lap of our journey, and what a task it was to do so. Sometimes I fancied that it might not be much more difficult to grow wings!

Eventually we made our departure. The truck was a closed affair and was piled high with luggage. We sat among the baggage as best we could while the dilapidated vehicle went bumping along for all it was worth, and it wasn't worth much. It broke down every now and then when a tire punctured or when the engine spluttered and refused to start again. Once we spent a whole day wandering near the roadside, while the driver went to a town about ten miles away to purchase some screws to replace those that had dropped off. Each day we started early in the morning and passed the night in a village that we happened to reach in the evening. The road wriggled along the side of hills and was often just a foot away from the edge of a precipice. The red laterite threw up a cloud of dust, but the sky was blue, the clouds were white, and the hills were green. Sometimes we came across a swarm of dragonflies sporting in the breeze. We spent three days in the truck, and it took us twenty days from the time we left the island of Hong Kong to arrive at Kukong.

Kukong, otherwise known as Shiukwan, was the wartime capital of Kwangtung, the provincial government having removed there after the collapse of Canton. Before we reached it, we had experienced violent storms, soaking rain, burning heat, hunger, and fatigue. One student had caught malaria, and most of us had fallen sick at some time or other. This place was the destination of our party, and here we separated. Some of the members stayed in this city while others traveled farther inland to different localities. Some students who were undergraduates proceeded to join various Chinese universities. I had obtained my degree, and my intention was to find a job.

Kukong was a straggling city of some extent with a few tolerable roads, the majority, however, being the usual narrow, cobbled lanes. The crowds were almost as thick as those in Hong Kong. The daily business began only at 2:00 PM, for air raids were practically confined to the mornings. The thought struck me that this was a distinct contrast from the practice in some lands where business took a siesta in the afternoons. The town was separated into two parts by a small river, the eastern section being the commercial area. There were several bridges spanning the river; the one that I had occasion to use mostly consisting of planks laid across a row of pontoons.

At night, when the electric lights diffused their dim radiance, the throngs in the streets were immense, sauntering and staring, hurrying and jostling. One of the most striking characteristics about China, forcibly bringing home its colossal population, consisted of the crowds surging in towns, however small. When one looked up a narrow street and beheld what appeared to be a solid mass of humanity, one might well be excused for wondering how it was possible to tread one's way through it.

I stayed in this town for a few days and spent the time wandering about the streets and the suburbs and sitting in the parks. After the oppressive atmosphere of Hong Kong, I felt it a relief to be there. Though planes passed through they dropped no bombs. Life appeared as normal as the abnormal war permitted. New roads and houses were continually being built, not of a durable kind maybe, but serviceable under the circumstances. The people might be poorly dressed, but they looked carefree. There were few beggars, and all seemed to have a sufficient amount of food to eat. Though

I was acquainted with scarcely anybody other than the former students of Hong Kong University in that wide expanse of war-stricken land, I felt no qualms about my not-too-pleasant situation.

One day I was sitting on a bench in the Chung Shan Park, about which there was nothing particularly noticeable. The weather was hot, and I was glad to be beneath the shade of trees. A man soon sauntered toward the bench and sat near me. We fell into conversation; on learning that I was a refugee from Hong Kong, he sympathized with my plight and uttered some words of hope and encouragement.

"I myself was not born in this town," he said. "I escaped from Canton on its fall. I was studying in Lingnan University and I went to Hong Kong. As you know, Lingnan University came to use the buildings of Hong Kong University. When I left Hong Kong, I came to Kukong, where I am teaching in a middle school. I presume you find life here hard." He looked at me inquiringly.

"It's better than what I have been experiencing for the last few months in Hong Kong," I said.

"Yes," he replied. "Whatever the life may be one feels free. That is more important than any material comfort."

"Undoubtedly," I responded with conviction, but with a tinge of speculation as to the length of time I could survive on freedom to the exclusion of concrete things.

"We can never lose the war," he averred. "We may be inferior in weapons and our soldiers may not be so well trained, but the vast extent of our territory, the great size of our population, and, above all, our will to resist make us unconquerable."

"What about traitors like Wang Ching-wei?"

"They are a disgrace, but it isn't likely that there will be many of that kind."

"What are the chances of recovering the occupied territories?"

"If the Pacific War had not broken out and China were to continue fighting the enemy alone, it would take a long time. I wouldn't have been able to forecast it. But you know time means little in the history of China where a period of turmoil could easily last for decades and even centuries. But when the Japanese attacked the Western countries, they were inviting their own destruction, for how could a small country eventually triumph over so many? I shouldn't think it would be many years before they are driven out," he said with conviction.

"What do you plan to do then?"

"I shall return to my native village. But I am not quite sure what I shall do."

"Are you married?"

"No. Difficult to marry in our present circumstances. I do not bother about whether life is hard or not. In fact, I am quite happy. But it is different when it comes to rearing a family. One doesn't want one's children to suffer."

"Of course," I agreed.

After sitting for some time longer, we parted. I returned to my lodgings, a dormitory that I occupied along with a score of others. The mosquitoes were quite numerous and, when they flew on their stinging missions, were as ferocious as human marauders. But we didn't bother about them, as we were equipped with adequate weapons of defense. Over each of our beds we hung a round mosquito curtain. Before dropping off to sleep, I reviewed my present circumstances and felt none too happy about my predicament, but resolved to worry as little as possible.

10. In a Train

I stayed in Kukong for five days and, there being no special reason for me to prolong my sojourn and wishing to go farther into the interior and see more of China, I departed with some of the friends who came with me from Hong Kong. We went to the railway station, and the train departed at 7:00 AM. We traveled along that stretch of the Canton-Hankow Railway still in Chinese hands. First we went northward toward Hengyang.

Surprisingly enough, the train was quite comfortable and not as crowded as I had imagined it would be. But a short while later it was forced to hide in a ravine for fear of an air raid, and we had to remain there for an hour and a half. The hills, which rose steeply on either side, were cloaked in green vegetation, but I saw no life of any kind, not even a bird. The place looked desolate, and I vaguely wondered whether it was made by nature specially to serve as a sanctuary for trains.

What a relief I felt when the train, which seemed to have gone to sleep forever, commenced to breathe, stretch itself, and move! It gathered momentum and we were on our way again. I fervently hoped that it would not prove the same as the truck and the boat, breaking down or stopping for one reason or another every now and then for an unconscionable length of time. My fears proved unfounded in that it turned out to be superior in performance to the other forms of conveyance—there being, for the duration of our journey, a few delays but not heartbreakingly so.

At 1:00 PM we reached Pengshek, a small town in which the Chung Shan University had taken its wartime abode. A precipitous rock stood near the railway station. The train rushed on without any mishap past villages and towns, and I watched the countryside flash its greenery. We were now journeying through the province of Hunan, and it was past midnight before we reached Hengyang, a key railway junction. We disembarked at the station, as we had to change trains. We took a boat to cross a river and thereafter walked for three miles to another railway station, from which the train for Kweilin started. We spent the rest of the night at this station sitting or sleeping on the floor.

I wandered about for some time outside the station. The moon was bright. I could hear dogs barking some distance away. Few people were about, and I felt the stillness of the night with all its mystery. The cool air was a pleasant change from the heat of the day. The houses in the vicinity were of wooden construction, and the stony roads were unusually rough. At the station the lights were dim lanterns, and I had to tread my way gingerly among the crowd of figures lying down amid their luggage. A sentry or two kept watch; they did not stand rigidly at attention rooted to some particular spot nor did they march up and down in a fixed fashion, but sauntered here and there in a leisurely manner.

Before dawn broke, the station began to come alive. A cough broke out here and there, and a child cried somewhere. The sleeping figures stirred and sat up, and before long people were moving about in unhurried activity. My friends and I went to a nearby matshed and had a breakfast of soy milk and twisted dough fritters. I looked around at the customers, who did not appear any the worse for sleeping at the railway station. They were not exactly merry but neither were there any grumblings. They just enjoyed their breakfast as much as we did ours. Most people appeared to travel in groups or with their families.

After we had our meal, we sauntered here and there awhile, the invigorating freshness of the morning air raising our spirits. The weather was fine and the clouds became whiter as the merry sun rose higher and higher above the horizon. Spirals of smoke ascended from the neighboring houses, and people hurried to and fro intent on their business. Looking at the peaceful scene, one would not think that the country was at war, although in fact the city had been receiving heavy pounding from air raids. When we returned to the railway station, people were already boarding the train, and we lost no time in following suit. As we sat in the carriage gazing out of the window, the most conspicuous sight was hefty Hunanese women calling vociferously for the passengers to drink their tea, each of them carrying a big pot and some bowls.

The train departed at 9:00 AM, traveling southwestward in the direction of Kwangsi Province. We did not encounter any untoward incident while we rolled along a wide plain past farmhouses built of mud, straggly villages, and crowded towns, past unpaved roads and turbid rivers. Some of the passengers fell asleep as the train thudded along while others were in a pensive mood. My friends and I engaged in desultory conversation, our principal topic being our present circumstances and our future plans.

"I am stopping in Kweilin for only a few days," remarked Fong Wai Sang, an engineering student. "I hope to be able to proceed to Chungking and enter a university there."

"I wonder whether I'll do that," said Ang Chuan Bee. "I have been told that the students there lead very miserable lives. The allowances they receive are very inadequate, they haven't enough to eat, and they do not even have proper books."

"Well, it can't be helped," said Wai Sang. He was a cheerful soul and was in the habit of looking at the bright side of things. "This is wartime. All I am concerned with is to get my degree. The hardships are nothing."

"I don't mind any troubles we may encounter," put in Lim Seh Huck, "but I think it's futile to pursue our studies here. I'll wait till the war is over. In the meantime I hope to be able to get a job."

"When is the war going to be over?" remarked Chuan Bee lugubriously.

There was no reply, for none of us knew the answer.

"What do you propose to do?" asked Saw Tek Chin, turning toward me. "You have got your degree. I don't suppose you want to continue your studies."

"I'll try and get a job in Kweilin," I remarked. "If I can't, I'll proceed to Chungking and see what I can do. I think it should not be too difficult for us to fend for ourselves."

"We are a real bunch of refugees," said Tek Chin with a laugh. "Soon I shall be forced to squat at the roadside with my things spread on the ground and sell them to get board and lodging."

We looked none too happy and cogitated over this problem of becoming vendors of our possessions, which were by no means bountiful.

"It's lucky that we have some things to sell," said Wai Sang. "When I was in Hong Kong, whatever spare cash I had over and above the estimated minimum traveling expenses I invested in goods, for we all knew before coming in of the inflation here and that it was better to bring in goods than cash."

"I can never forget the sentry, who took my things," remarked Chuan Bee with a look of anger on his face.

"I understand that even torn clothing can fetch a goodly sum," continued Wai Sang, not heeding the interruption. "I have a pair of trousers with a hole in it. I wonder how much I can get for it."

"Two hundred dollars, I should think," said Chuan Bee. "That is half the monthly salary of the average office worker in this place at present."

"Life is very hard here," grumbled Tek Chin. "When I was in Hong Kong I did not realize it would be so bad. People sleep four persons to a room, wear shabby clothing, eat mainly vegetables, and insufficient at that, and have no amusements of any sort. The way of life is primitive."

"Life may not be luxurious, but what of it?" said Wai Sang. "We were not well off in Hong Kong these last few months. I was living on rice and boiled soybeans. And I do not remember that I had any amusements."

"At any rate we are free," remarked Seh Huck. "We don't have to see the scowling faces of bad-tempered soldiers. You know, once when I was going back to my hostel I met a Japanese sentry. Unfortunately for me, I thought I would be polite and I therefore said, 'Ohayo.' The bastard immediately caught hold of me and turned me around and around, and raised his hand to slap me, but somehow desisted, shouted something, and let me go. I was quite mystified at his behavior until one day someone told me that 'ohayo' could only be used toward friends and inferiors. If one wanted to say 'good morning' to superiors, one should use the words 'ohayo gozaimasu.'"

We all laughed, and I said, "That comes of trying to show off a little learning, which, as is said, is a dangerous thing."

"I had an experience just as unpleasant," recalled Wai Sang. "I was walking along a poorly lit street one evening about nine o'clock when a Jap soldier, accompanied by a couple of Indian soldiers, came toward me, and suddenly torchlights were flashed in my face, and the Jap, who was staggering in drunkenness, laid both his filthy hands on my head. He muttered something and the Indians also said a few words to him. He then let go his hold on me. I think he mistook me for a girl!"

We laughed more loudly at this.

"A conquering army is a pest," I stated. "Every little soldier feels himself superior to any member of the conquered population. Wang Ching-wei may think that he is a ruler and a big shot, but I am sure that every Jap peasant in uniform in Nanking looks down on him as a member of an inferior race."

"We have escaped from a nightmare," said Seh Huck. "Whatever we may suffer here would be nothing compared to the indignities and dangers of living under the Japs."

We all nodded agreement, and there was a pause. I looked around at the passengers, most of whom appeared to be asleep while the rest were gazing listlessly out of the windows or talking in an apparently uninterested fashion. The train lumbered along. I turned my eyes toward the window and observed the farmers working in the fields, some with their backs bent and heedless of the passing train, while others straightened up to take a look and wipe the sweat from their brows.

My attention was suddenly recalled to my companions. "War is a terrible thing," Chuan Bee was saying. "Nothing but ruin and death. I never expected that I would have to undergo it."

"One's life is changed for the worse," responded Tek Chin, "if one is lucky enough not to be killed. I can't understand why people should want to go to war."

"I suppose countries fight for all sorts of reasons," said Wai Sang, "the main cause having always been the desire for more territory. But it does seem that whatever benefits an aggressor may get are not worth the carnage."

"I wonder how long this one is going to last," said Tek Chin with a wistful sigh.

"Modern wars don't last very long," I remarked, "but it is merely guesswork to say when it will end."

"I feel very concerned about my family in Singapore," said Seh Huck sadly. "You know, the Japs treated the people there horribly after its fall."

"Yes," agreed Tek Chin. "I have had no news about my folks in Kuala Lumpur. As far as we know, Malaya has had a worse time than Hong Kong. But what's the use of worrying? Our families are probably more worried about us, as we are alone away from home. Let us hope they will survive the ordeal; I dare say they will. You know, although war is so terrible, only a small percentage of combat personnel and a still smaller percentage of civilians actually perish."

"Is that so?" replied Chuan Bee. "I am glad to know this."

"I read it somewhere," stated Tek Chin. "At any rate, we won't be helping our families in any way by worrying. Our more urgent problem is to keep ourselves alive."

"It will be a happy day when we return home and find everybody safe and sound," said Wai Sang in sentimental mood.

"Look at the local people," I remarked. "They have gone through more years of war than one cares to count, yet they bear themselves stoically. Their fortitude is amazing. We should learn from them."

"Quite right," said Wai Sang. "I am ready for anything."

We all smiled and lapsed into silence

In the course of time, we crossed the border separating Kwangsi from Hunan and sped on toward our destination, Kweilin. The scenery changed; the terrain was no longer flat but rugged. Kwangsi is a plateau about two thousand feet high, bristling with steep hills flanking narrow valleys. We passed solitary limestone cliffs with strange shapes, and one could entertain oneself by fancying resemblances between them and diverse creatures or other things. It was well past midnight before the train rolled into Kweilin.

11. The Sino-Japanese War

Before proceeding further, I propose to review the Sino-Japanese War, tracing it to its origin, and to recount the history of the relations between the two countries. To begin at the beginning, we must go back to the war of 1894 when Japan first defeated China, then under the rule of the effete Manchus, and obtained Formosa as booty. The Japanese also gained a free hand in Korea, which until then was a Chinese tributary state. It was in this war that Japan first showed itself a modern military power. Unlike other Asian nations that tried to cling to their cultures as long as possible, it quickly adopted the material inventions of the West, for its imitative faculties far surpassed those of the others. The Western countries had been busily engaged in exploiting China but, owing to their mutual rivalries, had to content themselves with carving out spheres of influence. Japan now stepped into the picture and joined the other powers in this magnificent game. However, in its mind's eye, it was probably already dreaming of replacing the Manchus as the ruler of the whole country. For thousands of years the Mongolian peoples on the periphery of China cherished the ambition of dominating its lands; sometimes some particular tribe did actually succeed in subjugating the country in part or even in its entirety. The Manchus were one such tribe. Why shouldn't the Japanese be the new conquerors?

Because Russia's encroaching into Manchuria was a threat to its interests, Japan went to war against Russia and proved itself a really great power by defeating the Russians on Chinese territory. Japan then had sole influence in Manchuria. In the course of the First World War in 1915, the Japanese presented twenty-one demands to Yuan Shih-kai, the president of China, who was ambitious to found a new dynasty. Compliance with

71

these demands would have made China a vassal of Japan. Yuan Shih-kai accepted most of them but not the most serious ones. Soon thereafter, China entered the period of the warlords, and Japan was busy sowing discord and worsening the already existing state of confusion.

When Chiang Kai-shek led the Kuomintang to victory over the warlords and China appeared unified in 1928, the country could now be expected to embark on an era of peace and prosperity. This was not at all to the taste of the Japanese, who saw their dream of conquest threatened. Unfortunately for China, along with the inventions of the West, its ideologies had surged, including communism. Chiang Kai-shek detested communism, and he considered it imperative to destroy the communists first before going to war against a foreign enemy. He waged campaign after campaign against them until they were dislodged from their stronghold in Kiangsi Province, but they then made the historic trek to Northwest China and got an even better stronghold in Yenan. In the meantime, the Japanese were free to tighten their stranglehold on China.

In 1931, on the pretext of a railway incident, the Japanese seized Manchuria and installed the last emperor of China, Pu-yi, as emperor of the supposedly independent state of Manchukuo. As in modern warfare it had become fashionable to pretend that aggression was really carried out as an act of self-defense, the so-called Kwantung army, the vanguard of Japanese imperialism, had contrived to stage an incident on the night of September 18, 1931, by blowing up a section of the railway in the Mukden area. They then attributed the dynamiting to the Chinese soldiers quartered in a nearby barracks and claimed that their patrol had been attacked by these same troops. The upshot of the business was that they occupied Mukden and eventually all Manchuria.

Emboldened by its facile conquest, Japan proceeded to extend its power into North China by manufacturing an incident just as it did in Manchuria. On the night of July 7, 1937, near the Marco Polo Bridge twelve miles south of Peking (then known as Peiping), Japanese troops were alleged to have been fired on by Chinese soldiers. Thereupon the Japanese Army launched an offensive of such a nature that it could only have been prepared in advance. They occupied Peking and Tientsin, but by this time Chiang Kai-shek had decided that it was time to make a determined stand against them. Japanese naval and army units attacked Shanghai, which was staunchly defended for almost three months before it fell. The enemy then captured the capital, Nanking, on November 9. They took Hankow and

Canton a year later and thus came into possession of East China, sealing off all supplies to the country by sea.

Chiang Kai-shek retreated to Chungking in the mountainous province of Szechwan on the upper reaches of the Yangtze River. Here he waged his War of Resistance. There were also the Communists under Mao Tse-tung who initiated guerilla warfare against the common enemy. For the next few years there was little large-scale fighting, and the war became almost a stalemate. Japan could not advance much further, but the Chungking government fell into increasing difficulties. The Japanese could not subdue Chungking, for their navy would have to traverse tortuous gorges against rapid currents while their armies would have to cross mountains and move in a region devoid of roads and railways. Aerial attacks could only harass but could not subjugate the city. They did indeed contrive to capture a few more cities, including Nanchang, capital of Kiangsi, in 1939 and Ichang below the gorges of the Yangtze in 1940. But they could not destroy the Nationalist government or the Communists directed by Yenan.

However, what was called Free China was being strangled economically. The loss of the seaports, the big cities, and the rich lands as well as the difficulty of obtaining supplies from the outside world were seriously suffocating it. At first supplies arrived via Burma Road, and when this was closed, they were flown over the snow-clad Himalayas to Kunming. But they were grossly insufficient, and when American forces came to China, they were intended mainly for them. A sign of the deteriorating economic situation was the rapid inflation caused by the mounting cost of the war, the lack of adequate revenue, and the scarcity of goods.

With their inability to annihilate completely the Chiang Kai-shek government by military means, the Japanese had recourse to other methods but without any more attractive results. Besides the policy of economic strangulation, they resorted to the expedient of setting up puppet regimes and established such governments in Peking, Nanking, and Canton, the chief of these being at Nanking under Wang Ching-wei. They hoped that the Chinese would rally around Wang Ching-wei and desert Chiang Kai-shek but, of course, no such phenomenon materialized. The case of Wang Ching-wei, a close disciple of Sun Yat-sen and an ardent Nationalist and Republican revolutionary, shows how human beings can change their behavior under the potent stress of jealousy. He looked at Chiang Kai-shek with a jaundiced eye. As the senior associate of the founder of the Kuomintang, he considered that the leadership of the country and party should have devolved on him. It is because of men such as Wang Ching-wei, who willingly collaborate with a conqueror, that a country can become really subjugated. To be defeated in battle is bad enough; to be defeated in the mind is worse.

Let us pause a little to consider the holocaust. Was war between China and Japan inevitable? Japan was out to conquer China—there could be no doubt of that. It started off its modern career by defeating China in Korea and, until 1941, engaged in war almost exclusively against China. The main exception was the war against Russia, incited by their rivalry in Manchuria; that is, the contest was about Chinese territory. How could China do other than fight back? That it took such a long time to do so, that it could indulge in civil war, that the Nationalists and the Communists feared one another more than they hated the common enemy, that there were sections of the people who ostensibly collaborated with the Japanese—all this would be astounding if we did not know from history that under certain circumstances the inhabitants of a country could behave in such an irrational way as to give rise to the impression that they preferred foreign domination.

That the Chinese were defeated by the Japanese when the full-scale invasion came in 1937 and, in a short time, lost half the country would be strange if we considered only the relative sizes of the two countries and their populations. In fact, nobody expected China to be able to withstand Japan, and people thought it heroic that Shanghai took three months to succumb. The trouble was that because China had been demoralized and weakened by a century of foreign aggression, by the 1930s it was not in a position to fight properly. Its air force was small, the Japanese destroyed it in no time, and their planes could then roam over the land doing whatever they pleased. Its navy was insignificant, for in spite of decades of aggression from the sea, the Chinese still thought in terms of invasion by land. Its armies, though large, were badly equipped.

It must not be forgotten that the general war in China initiated by the Marco Polo Bridge incident in 1937 extended over a longer period of time than the Second World War and that for four years the Chinese fought alone. When war erupted in Europe in 1939, the two areas of conflict had no connection with each other. After Japan bombed Pearl Harbor in December 1941, the Chinese scene became involved with the wider world arena. But even then, though theoretically its struggle was part and parcel of the Allied cause, it received little aid, as the European theater was deemed vastly more important. American supplies came over "the hump" along with planes flown by the Americans themselves, but these were meager and were intended just to save China from what was feared would inevitably be an unmitigated collapse if left to its own resources.

Weak as China was, it was aware right from the beginning that its chance for survival was to trade time for space, to weary the enemy and lengthen their lines of communication, to force them to stay mired in the mud and wear down their resources and morale. It is a moot point for how long China could have withstood Japan and whether it would have eventually succumbed, had Japan not been dramatically defeated by the Allies. Even if the Nationalists, entrenched in Szechwan, which was inaccessible to the Japanese, had capitulated, it was unlikely that the Communists would have given up. Doubtless their guerilla warfare would have continued for many more years to come. However, speculating over historical possibilities is a futile exercise.

The government attempted reconstruction of the free areas. Industries were launched with machinery brought in from factories dismantled before the cities were abandoned and small ones organized as cooperatives were developed. Highways were built of water-bound macadam and, though far from technical perfection, were at least serviceable. Education, which had traditionally been held in high esteem, continued to play its important role. The famous universities, formerly located in the cities that had fallen to the enemy, had moved inland, the students and their teachers taking with them the needed equipment and continuing the studies amid appalling conditions. This development of the interior was one beneficial result of the war.

It would not be amiss to reflect a little on war in general. There have historically been several kinds. Setting aside civil wars and considering only foreign wars, there is the war of naked aggression when an ambitious ruler unashamedly sets out to conquer and annex another country. There is the war of incidental expansion in which a country, without deliberately seeking it, fights against a neighbor due to a variety of causes, including natural quarrelsomeness, self-defense, rivalry, and whatnot and, emerging victorious, extends its territorial boundaries. There is the ideological war, by which a people considers that—for the preservation of its own existence or for the glorification of its culture or for the sake of bringing light to the benighted—it should endeavor to export its ideas by force. There is the war of freedom when a subject people rises up to emancipate its territory from rulers of another race.

From whatever cause a war arises, in the ultimate analysis, it means the capture of territory. Each side either gains, loses, succeeds in maintaining, or fails to capture territory. This desire for land is, of course, inherent in human nature. Man is also born with a pugnacious instinct. The acquisitive plus the pugnacious instincts led primitive man to war. The rise of civilization did not eliminate it, but as time went on, thinkers did influence large sections of people to condemn it. It has persisted to the present day. In fact, owing to technological development, it has become more frightful than ever. It is not quite true to say that in former ages it was a matter of battles between armies, and civilians were not involved, for towns were besieged and sacked and whole populations vanished. Then, as now, victorious armies behaved atrociously toward subjugated inhabitants. But the plane and rocket and the concept of total war have brought all the denizens of a country within the arena of dire conflict.

Is there any justification for war? None for the aggressive type concerned purely with territorial acquisition. It is no excuse to allege that a nation requires to expand because of its population explosion, or because it needs raw materials for its factories or markets for its manufactures, or because it requires a buffer state to protect it against enemies. Why should it be right for it to attain these objectives to the detriment of its neighbors? In the case of war for other purposes, like the promotion of an ideology, even if they were not merely masks to cover territorial greed, it too has little justification, though it may not be so evil. As regards defensive war, the right ends with the expulsion of the aggressor; it does not extend to annexing his domains in retaliation.

Cruelty and waste are the twin peaks of war. Its destruction of property, its loss of lives, and above all its bestial cruelty make it completely abhorrent, an undiluted curse. Apologists have tried to extol its supposed virtues, including fortitude, comradeship, bravery, and selflessness, but surely these can be bred in other ways than in a holocaust. Actually, these qualities are not universal in war, and there is just as much, if not more, of the opposite kind. However, if these virtues come into being only through war and can be found nowhere else, the price paid for them would be too high. To fight to live may be justifiable; to live to fight is barbaric. War nowadays, with its vastly more destructive weapons, is much more terrifying than before. Above all, the nuclear threat, with its capacity for wiping out the human race, makes it unthinkable.

Whether war will ever cease altogether is doubtful. We may condemn it, descant on its irrationality, waste, and cruelty, and shiver at the prospect of the resort to nuclear weapons, but there is no certainty that it will not persist, human nature being what it is. Measures have been devised to make it more humanitarian, but in the heat of battle they have been easily violated. Plans have been made to interdict it, but it is still far from being extinct. However, there is no need to lose hope. With the ever-growing interdependence of the peoples of the world, it may vanish and pass into the limbo of oblivion.

Coming back to the Sino-Japanese War, it was in the worst category: that of pure aggression for the purpose of annexing another country for exploitation. There was not even any question of ideology, and it had nothing to justify it. The aggression was deliberate and was pursued with a dogged persistence for half a century. The general war, which commenced in 1937, was merely the culminating point of a long process. The conflict was an unmitigated tragedy to the most populous of countries, and it was conducted by the Japanese with unsurpassed cruelty and disregard of the rules of modern warfare. It was a devastating storm without meaning, even for the invaders. When it ended, the Japanese had failed to attain their objective. They would have done better not to have initiated it.

12. Life in Kweilin

Kweilin was the capital of the province of Kwangsi. Its natural scenery was superb, as expressed in the popular saying that it was the best in the world. Its craggy limestone hills of weird shapes contained innumerable caves, the most celebrated of the hills bearing the romantic appellation of the Seven Star Crags. The gloomy caves were a veritable maze of passages with strange figures formed by dripping water impregnated with lime. The city was traversed by the Kwei River with its green water lapping black rocks.

The town was originally engirdled by a wall of which remnants still stood, including the customary four gates. Its two main roads, which were fairly wide and lined with trees, intersected at its center; the lengthy one, running north and south, was a very busy street and, especially in the evenings, was crowded to congestion by pedestrians. It had not been modernized to any considerable extent. Nearly all buildings were of two stories and of wooden construction, and there were few motorcars, the principal vehicles being rickshaws and wheelbarrows.

When I first arrived at the place, I found accommodation in a hostel built and run by the provincial government for the benefit of overseas Chinese, the rent being comparatively lower than at commercial lodging houses. The two-story building was made of timber and built around a central courtyard. The rooms on the upper floor opened onto a gallery from which one looked down on the courtyard. The ground floor was not paved but was made of consolidated earth.

The heat of summer was terrific, worse than anything I had ever experienced in Malaya, and one sweated with the greatest of ease. Water was precious, and in the hostel I had to pay for a cold bath carried out with a single pail of water. Life could not be said to be easy; every necessity and luxury was at a minimum. However, Kweilin was situated in a fertile district and was not far from Hunan, the rice bowl of China, so there was no perceptible scarcity of rice, which formed the staple food of the southerners. The northerners subsisted on wheat, making it into a kind of bread, termed *mantou*. Things seemed as though it was peacetime. There were few soldiers visible and no curfews. Only the air-raid alarms, which might or might not be succeeded by bombings, made one sense the atmosphere of war; during the alerts, all movement along the roads was prohibited.

I tramped the streets looking for work and imbibed prodigious quantities of tea as a result of the heat and fatigue. After staying in Kweilin for about three weeks, I found a job. I came to know an engineer who introduced me to the head of a road construction office, and I was appointed to an engineering post. It so happened that a university friend of mine, also from Malaya, by the name of Lee Poon, was in Kweilin at the time. He had left Hong Kong but not in my party. He too was taken into the same office, and we started work at the same time.

This job ensured that I had a place to stay in and that I was not destined to starve to death. It also terminated my travels for the time being at least. The first thing I had to do was remove my abode from the lodging house to a hostel provided for the staff.

This building was near the office, which was located on the outskirts of the town, and was of the usual wooden, two-story type. Bachelors normally had to stay three or four persons to a room. I shared one on the upper floor with Lee Poon and another person, who incidentally was addicted to Peking opera; every evening he would sing loudly extracts from plays to the accompaniment of his screeching fiddle. He sang the female parts as well in a high falsetto that made me shiver. The room that we occupied was bare of all furniture save our three beds together with their appurtenances, including mosquito curtains and quilts stuffed with cotton wool. We, of course, had with us our baggage, which contained all our worldly possessions.

Life in the hostel was not in the least exhilarating, but it was not intolerable to us. No amenities or amusements of any sort were available, and there was no common room where the residents could gather. The hostel was just a collection of bedrooms with each inmate occupying a corner of one, and that was all his interest in it. There were, however, servants to sweep the rooms occasionally. As there were also women who took in washing, we didn't have to do this chore. There being no electric lights but only flickering oil lamps, it was a strain to read at night. There was nothing to do but to sleep early if one did not go out of the hostel in the evening. Our life would not have been described by one living in an affluent society as comfortable, but we did not feel distressed. We had few necessities, for a necessity is what one can get.

For meals, the office had a mess hall located in a room on the ground floor of its premises. Those who joined it had to go out with the cook to the market in the morning to purchase the required foodstuffs. Meat was expensive, and our food consisted almost entirely of diverse kinds of vegetables and vegetable derivatives, such as bean curd. We had three meals a day at 6:30 AM, 11:00 AM, and 4:30 PM. The food was quite sufficient and we didn't go hungry.

The office where I was employed was divided into different sections, each devoted to one category of work. Mine was the design section, where engineering schemes were planned and designed and drawings made. Office hours were from 7:00 AM to 11:00 AM and 1:30 PM to 4:30 PM daily, except Sundays when we had the afternoon off. There were only five public holidays in a year: New Year's Day of the solar calendar, the birthday of Sun Yat-sen, Confucius's birthday, Commemoration Day of the Seventy-Two Heroes, and the Double Tenth or the Foundation Day of the Republic. However, it did not mean that we were ardently engaged in unremitting toil. The employees sauntered into the office half an hour late. It was common to see them chattering away as though that was their occupation, and some were even busy playing chess or checkers. In fact, the work was performed at a leisurely pace.

My colleagues were friendly and helpful right from the start. I did not sense the slightest hostility from them because I was a stranger. I was treated as one of them. The relations among themselves were quite good, and I never saw them quarrel. The war and poverty did not exacerbate their tempers and tongues and make them forget their manners. They seldom talked of the war but conducted themselves as though the life they led was normal. Now and then I did hear someone grumble slightly at the high cost of living, but they were not addicted to perpetual complaints of inadequate incomes and how to extract more money from their employers. They did not laugh merrily, neither did they show any gloom. They just carried on living from hand to mouth without any excitement or fuss.

Inflation was already quite serious but very far from the astronomical heights it was to attain later. Prices rose continually, and none of us would dream of keeping money; presumably, even misers did not love the sight of currency notes. If we had any cash to save, and that was precious little, we immediately converted it into goods. The cheapest of locally made shirts cost $80 in October 1942, and a pair of shoes, which wore out with surprising rapidity, $120. An alarm clock which I bought in Hong Kong in 1939 for $5, I sold in January 1943 for $500. The government made attempts to halt the incessant increase in prices but without the slightest effect.

The restaurants did a flourishing business. It seems an odd thing that when there is general distress in a country, be it an economic depression in peacetime or a war, restaurants as well as places of entertainment do not appear to flourish to any considerably lesser extent. The government passed sumptuary laws to restrict eating in such places; restaurateurs and customers were fined if, say, three persons shared more than two dishes of meat plus one of soup. But there were curious ways of evasion, such as supplying bigger dishes, removing an empty dish the moment it was finished and replacing it with another, and flitting from eating house to eating house. Gendarmes seemed to have nothing better to do than to visit restaurants to catch culprits; should anyone be found violating the legal measures, he was made to stand on a chair in full view of the other customers while the officer gave him a lecture in a loud, impressive voice on the immorality of excessive eating in wartime.

There were two newspapers published in Kweilin, each consisting of only one sheet of coarse paper. Though the print was a strain on the eyes, it was clearer than the books issued then. In spite of the one sheet, there were still a lot of advertisements. As the press was controlled, it spoke the official views. Although sometimes there was a spate of thefts, robberies, and murders, the newspapers rarely referred to them, for frequent and lurid accounts of them were construed as reflecting on the competence of the local authorities!

There were cinemas showing Hollywood movies, but the apparatus was so worn out that the pictures were blurred and the sounds indistinct. Worst of all, the mechanism broke down with regular frequency so that the audience had to sit patiently for the show to resume; it was rare for a picture to be uninterrupted from beginning to end. Sometimes the apparatus refused to start altogether and, after sitting for a long time, the patrons had to leave and then the money was refunded. Even so, crowds flocked to the theaters.

Life was simple not by choice but from necessity. All conveniences and luxuries, if they existed at all, were so costly as to be beyond the reach of nearly everybody. Clothing was coarse, and shabby Western-style suits were worn only by gentlemen. But they were a scream, and in normal times most of them would have been discarded as unfit for further use. Ladies did not talk of the latest fashion in dress. The number of private cars in the streets could be counted on one's fingers. Scarcely anybody could take pride in a well-kept home, for there were practically no gadgets or delicate furniture to adorn it. Life was pretty stark, although the newspapers sometimes lamented the modernization and luxuriousness of Kweilin owing to the great influx of refugees. They saw evil in the change from simplicity and frugality to ostentation and waste.

It was laughable to imagine that there was any superfluity of luxuries there, but presumably it was considered ostentatious to have such things as cinemas, Western-style suits, and cars. Then, of course, there were the restaurants, which sprang up like mushrooms serving the various styles of Chinese cuisine. Furthermore, wine was freely sold, this not being the case in other provinces. Kweilin had no museums but possessed a miserable library with a few books, and it did not have any good parks.

While the heat of summer was vexatious, when winter came it was quite cold. South China, for its position in the vicinity of the Tropic of Cancer, exhibits a low winter temperature; snow and ice are indeed rare, but the thermometer often hovers not many degrees above the freezing point. I woke up one morning in January to find a thin layer of ice covering the bottom of my washbasin. Braziers with burning lumps of charcoal provided a modicum of heat, and hawkers carried small pots, framed into bamboo baskets and containing some glimmering embers embedded in ashes, to warm themselves. Often rain fell for days on end, not in torrents but in steady drizzles, and the roads were converted into thick layers of red mud. When winter ended, summer began, for no real spring, blithe and mild, unmistakably adorned the year.

There was, however, one place where spring was said to be spring, and that was Yao Shan, a hill about a dozen kilometers from Kweilin. With some of my colleagues I walked for more than two hours through the beautiful countryside to that locality. The brown hill was low and was covered with verdant grass but possessed hardly any trees. At its foot, gambling booths and hawkers' stalls were much in evidence, and dense crowds of sightseers were assembled. Schools were even closed to allow the boys and girls to go there to enjoy the spring. At the top was a temple where daily hordes of the devout came to worship. The glory of this hill was the azaleas, which bloomed in profusion, the small crimson flowers presenting an enchanting spectacle.

The Western solar calendar had been adopted officially, and its New Year was one of the public holidays. But the celebration had political overtones, the national flag fluttering from many a window. It was largely ignored by the populace and most of the shops remained open. In our office, the occasion was marked by a dinner when each of us brought a gift generally wrapped up. All the packages were numbered and lots drawn; in this way, gifts were exchanged. The lunar New Year, whose name was officially changed to the Spring Festival, continued to exercise its fascination over the people and was jubilantly observed with the traditional color and éclat. Shops closed for days on end, there was the customary atmosphere of gaiety, and crackers resounded incessantly. On January 11, 1943, the United States and the United Kingdom signed treaties with China abolishing extraterritoriality. This signified that they relinquished their special status in China, their nationals would be subject to Chinese law, and their enclaves in the treaty ports would pass out of their hands. The government decreed that the celebration of this termination of the age-old Unequal Treaties should be held in the Chinese New Year season, the first three days of the lunar year that fell on February 5, 6, and 7 being declared public holidays. Meetings, lantern processions, and lion dances abounded. A political celebration was thus added to the traditional festivities.

Air-raid alarms were frequent, though they were not often followed by actual onslaughts. They were given in a number of towns simultaneously; enemy planes might even fly past on their way to other places. An elaborate system of warnings was practiced. When a raid might be expected, a lantern, which at night shone like a red ball, was hoisted up a pole on the top of a hill. When the attacking craft had come within a certain radius, another appeared to be immediately followed by the sound of the siren rising and falling in long waves. An urgent signal might ensue when the siren emitted a succession of short blasts, rapidly swelling and subsiding in piercing screams, and the two lanterns were hauled down. All doors were shut and silence reigned in the deserted streets. Right from the initial warning, the populace commenced to stream into the suburbs to ensconce themselves in the caves; with the last signal, late stragglers ran. Unless the bombers were actually overhead, the prevalent atmosphere suggested a picnic. The participants wandered about the countryside inhaling the fresh air, indulging in joyous converse, and even eating, for hawkers plied a vigorous trade. It might seem queer that the hawkers should have cared to bear along with them their ponderous loads, but apparently it was easier to do so than convey them back to their homes. Besides, business was business. The appearance of planes, the burst of a bomb, the crackle of anti-aircraft fire—these punctuated the long, monotonous intervals of the alert. The damage was generally not of great consequence, and the small bombs often landed on empty ground. Indeed, most people were acclimatized to raids and were so little concerned that a face stricken with terror or excitement was a rarity. Though, occasionally a house caught fire or a casualty was reported. When the Japanese had retreated a certain distance, both the lanterns reappeared, and those persons who had been fretting for several hours to return to their homes chattered volubly in expectation of the final signal. As a rule, soon afterward the siren gave vent to a glad note of relief as the lanterns were hauled down. The raid was over. The inhabitants flocked back into the city, reopened their shops, and resumed the tasks they had been compelled to relinquish temporarily; the attack was promptly forgotten.

A remarkable phenomenon was the apparently normal life of the ordinary householder, as though no war was afoot. Certainly, inflation, air raids, slogans on walls and posts, and troops of soldiers were evidence that affairs were not absolutely normal. Nevertheless, as one commonplace day succeeded another and people went about their diurnal tasks in a matter-of-fact manner and had their occasional small enjoyments, the feeling predominated that there was nothing amiss. Unless the battle was at the doorstep, it was convenient to ignore it, convenient and good for endurance, as a perennial state of stress and strain could never carry the people through a prolonged conflict. A nation of greater military strength (but more high-strung) would have collapsed after a series of disastrous defeats, culminating in the loss of half the land and leaving a deadly blockade, severely depleted resources, and towns of timber buildings.

I stayed in Kweilin for nearly ten months. I could write to friends in Hong Kong and obtain occasional news. Curiously enough, there was a postal service still in operation between free and occupied territory, though delivery was uncertain. The borderline between the two regions was unstable, and people were continually crossing and recrossing it. Under such circumstances, smuggling and espionage could present few difficulties, the peril being apparently inconsiderable.

13. Liuchow

The director of my office in Kweilin secured another job, to wit, the construction of an airfield at Liuchow. The preliminary survey of the site was to be undertaken by a party of men from my place, and I was chosen to be among the number. We left by train in May 1943 and worked in Liuchow for a fortnight. We had to toil daily from 6:00 AM to 6:00 PM and walked the distance of two kilometers from our lodging house to the work site. We were exposed alternately to the violent rays of the sun and vehement downpours of rain. I felt so exhausted on returning in the evening to the lodging house—which, unattractive externally, was miserable internally—that I could hardly climb onto my bed. We traced the journey back to Kweilin, but the following month I was permanently transferred along with half the staff of our office to Liuchow.

Liuchow was about one hundred miles to the southwest of Kweilin in the same province; it was not so populous and could scarcely be eulogized as fine. The town was clustered on the northern and southern banks of the Liu Kiang River, and was connected by a pontoon bridge. Liuchow bore a curious reputation—for coffins, exceedingly prized on account of the high quality of the wood in the vicinity. A popular saying stated: "Live in Hangchow, die in Liuchow." Some folks might deem it a dubious privilege to dwell in such a spot!

In spite of its unprepossessing specialty, it displayed the characteristics of a typical town. Situated far to the south, it lay along the railway line that ran westward from Hunan to Kweichow and on a tributary of the Si Kiang, which flows eastward down to Canton. Its climate is mild, though in winter it can be severely cold, especially around the time of the commencement of the lunar year. Rain is abundant and is not confined to any particular season. Its most noted natural object is a low peak, bearing the name of the Standing Fish from its faint resemblance to that phenomenon. The summit was occupied by an air-raid alarm station, and at the foot were located government offices. Its houses were of brick or timber, erected without any pretensions to architectural glory. The streets were constructed of broken stone bound by earth so that when the sun shone, bright clouds of dust were whipped up by passing vehicles and, when rain fell in showers, the mud, six inches thick, encrusted shoes and trousers. Electricity was provided but, the power being small, the lights were none of the most brilliant. Water was carried in wooden buckets on shoulder-poles from the river.

Moored to the northern side of the river near the center of the town were four big old junks, which had two decks each and were connected to one another by gangways. They were put to use as a teahouse, which was lit by numerous oil lamps, and formed against the dark background a brilliant spectacle at night. They also achieved great popularity, accounted for partly by the cool breezes disporting through them. The center of each boat contained a number of open rooms, while the sides were lined with small, wooden tables. Tea cost one dollar per person when I first went there, and a plate of snacks from three to four dollars. The waiters (there were no waitresses) wore white livery.

In June, when I arrived in Liuchow for the second time, the rain descended in torrents day after day. The river became so swollen that the pontoon bridge was removed and the crossing was made in boats. One morning a tragedy occurred. A big raft towed by a steamer was about to start from the south side of the river when it collapsed under its terrific load of about four hundred passengers. Several scores of people, mostly children, on their way to school, were drowned. The river continued to swell until it overflowed both banks, and the road bordering the northern bank was inundated with the water reaching up to the second story of the three-story houses. Thousands were rendered homeless. This flood, one of the worst in the history of the town, succeeded a prolonged drought.

I shifted my quarters several times. At first I occupied a room on the unpaved ground floor of a new three-story building, which was partly our field office and partly quarters. Then I lived on the second floor of a former lodging house, the only good point here being that I was allocated a small room wholly to myself. I changed quarters because I was transferred to our main office, which was located in a big hotel in town. Then when the office came under different control, a new director having been appointed, the place of work was also removed to a building in the suburbs. A bit nearer the airfield, the building was the ceremonial hall of a school. While we worked we could see the boys at play. A few months later, I shifted to a new house opposite a market where I stayed in a big room on the front part of the second floor. It admitted light through five glass tiles on the roof but was not provided with any windows for fresh air. I shared the room with an office mate. Finally, shortly before my departure from Liuchow, troops requisitioned this building, and my friend and I removed to a hut opposite our office, consisting of a floor of beaten earth with three small rooms. But we two enjoyed the glory of occupying the whole house.

At the time I was transferred to the Liuchow Airfield Construction Office, the chief engineer (called director) was a man named Lo Ying. After only four or five months at this job, which he held concurrently with the one in Kweilin, he was dismissed from it. The directorship of the Liuchow office was taken over by one Tsou Yo Sheng. War or no war, office grabbing was still very much in fashion. When an office changed chiefs the existing staff, as was the practice, automatically had their services terminated. But as the new director did not have enough men of his own, a number of officers, including myself, were retained. So I continued with my work in Liuchow.

The Liuchow airfield was one of the airfields being constructed in Free China for the use of the United States Air Force. These airfields were meant for military purposes only and were planned to be completed in a matter of months. Furthermore, there were no imported materials, such as bitumen to be used for runways, or sophisticated machinery, such as bulldozers or steamrollers, available. The runways were made of water-bound macadam consisting of local limestone blocks and chippings, the cementing material being red earth. As in the case of public roads, in the event of rain the earth became mud. It was manpower that built these airfields; literally thousands of men worked in an area, transporting stone and earth in wheelbarrows and baskets and dragging heavy rollers. There were, of course, buildings for various purposes, including control towers, offices, and barracks, all made of timber, rough-and-ready structures for temporary use. From these airfields American planes took off to unload their bombs on enemy targets, including Japan itself.

I found life in Liuchow much the same as in Kweilin. People ate, reared their families, and went about their ordinary business as though war was just a historical drama enacted on the stage and without any relevance to actual life. Restaurants flourished and sumptuary laws had no effect.

One regulation that came into being required a person not to order more than $50 for a meal or $15 for refreshments. At that time a small plate of fish or chicken cost $35, and it was difficult to have even two dishes for a meal. A cup of coffee cost $15, so for refreshments one could have coffee without anything to eat. Alternatively, one could have Chinese tea for $2 plus three plates of snacks at $4 per plate and containing two small pieces each. I was amazed as to why the government did not resort to rationing foodstuffs instead of experimenting with one method after another to limit consumption in restaurants, which at the very worst could not utilize more than a fraction of the total quantity of food eaten. Instead of being aimed at the promotion of national strength or the husbanding of material resources, its actions seemed to be merely killjoy in intent. The cinemas, which were even worse than those in Kweilin—the apparatus more subject to breakdowns and the sound and vision more blurred—drew crowds in spite of their appalling defects.

During the first year of my stay in Liuchow, air-raid alarms were not rare, but hardly any planes ever made their appearance. During an alert the inhabitants fled to the suburbs and hillsides, and all shops were closed. The streets were deserted save for policemen who patrolled them with guns. It was not until Liuchow was about to be invaded that real air raids occurred. These, which were frequent, often took place at night. A favorite target was the airfield. Explosive and incendiary bombs were employed, and sometimes the darkness was illuminated by crimson fires. I had a nasty experience one night after hearing the first bombing. I was in the act of opening the door of the hut where I was staying to walk across the road to a safer place when a bomb fell about fifty yards away. The tiles and boards of my ramshackle dwelling were shattered by the blast, and dust and fragments dropped freely on my head. After a while I gingerly opened the door and surveyed the scene. Smoke filled the roadway. One wing of a school building that was hit by the bomb was totally annihilated. A workman standing in a pit nearby had his face severely battered. In the distance, red flames soared to the skies from the airfield, where gasoline stores had been struck.

What I am going to describe for the remainder of this chapter applies not just to Liuchow but to Kweilin and other towns in Free China as well. Life was not pleasant as far as material conveniences went. The severe dearth of goods entailed by the blockade, which sealed the country from Manchuria to Yunnan, made luxuries of ordinary foreign articles. As the price level soared, less and less money was available for education and recreation, the cost of food swallowing up the income. Civil servants lodged in hostels provided for them free of rent, took their meals at a mess hall, and bought some of their commodities at the cooperative stores that each office organized.

Coarse cotton cloth of a blue color was the common fabric for wearing apparel, while better material was extremely scarce. Clothing was simple, and there was no question of elegance. Boys and girls in schools all wore uniforms. In winter, woolen suits or long gowns lined with fur were in evidence. But what was far more prevalent was the coat, padded with cotton wool, much favored as a preserver of heat. It was also utilized in the making of quilts. They were indispensable on a cold night and merely consisted of a thick layer of the downy material snugly interposed between sheets of cloth.

Education had always held the supreme place of esteem in the middle nation. From ancient times scholars were reverenced. After the abolition of feudalism more than two thousand years ago and the institution of a civil service, learning formed the best passport to office, though unfortunately this did not preclude widespread illiteracy. The educated, in the dire absence of ordinary pleasures that had become expensive, were even more devoted to their books than before. Old volumes were greatly treasured, as printing costs were prohibitive and new publications were of slender size, mostly for the use of students.

Paper was the coarsest imaginable, of a pallid hue bearing print well-nigh illegible and a strain to the eyes. Bookshops were plentiful, though the turnover could not be considerable, as numerous readers crossed their thresholds not to make purchases but to enjoy a free treat; a rapid peruser could without much difficulty contrive to finish a good many publications. A newspaper comprised a single sheet, largely imparting political news. Glancing through the advertisements one was struck by the tremendous number of losses of badges and certificates, for it was a rule to notify publicly that the missing article was thenceforth to be null and void.

Working hours were long, the day commencing early in the morning. As mechanical appliances were at a minimum, strenuous muscular labor, as in medieval times, was perforce at a maximum. The water carriers, who were such a prominent feature, the porters who bore heavy loads on their shoulders, the boatmen rowing with might and main, the farmers who toiled incessantly—what an expenditure of energy! Work can be extremely exhilarating, but not toil involving such a bitter amount of physical exhaustion. However, it was carried out with stoic resignation.

The transport problem bristled with difficulties. There were the usual rickshaws, far from adequate in number, and hence charging excessive fares. Save for a very few for official uses, the motor vehicles were all trucks, which were always overloaded and in dilapidated condition, lumbering along slowly and breaking down frequently. They were not numerous either; even a seat in them was not easily obtainable and cost an exorbitant sum. In the rivers plied the boats that could be used for crossing ferries or covering long distances. In the circumstances, it naturally came to pass that the traffic was almost entirely pedestrian, and excursions to other localities for pleasure were unknown.

The most facile method for making money was by speculation. Truck drivers amassed fortunes, taking advantage of the exigencies of travelers and surreptitiously conveying goods from a cheaper area to a dearer. The chief economic victims of the troublous times were the educated, who found themselves earning a miserable pittance as salaried functionaries. As a whole, the real wages of labor deviated but slightly from the prewar rate. The currency, which rapidly deteriorated, was no longer kept as savings, gold taking its place in this respect.

The life of the soldier was the severest in the world, and the shortage of supplies was appalling. It might legitimately engender wonder as to how the troops failed to collapse altogether under such adverse conditions. Long distances were traversed on foot. Poorly equipped armies had to be pitted against the ruthlessness of a foe by whom the art of war was cultivated with insensate enthusiasm. It was not strange that there should have been many reverses; it was strange that the task of resistance was maintained year after year. It was performed by sheer dogged determination, born of consciousness of right. Nowadays war has become a creature of science, but battle-proud aggressors, relying on their instruments of murder, should beware of moral anger, for there is still room for an unconquerable will.

Despite the unfavorable conditions and paucity of facilities, there existed a certain measure of sober happiness. Luxuries are not the necessary constituents of content, and even a low material standard of living can be cheerfully borne on behalf of a sound cause that demands sacrifices. It is curious how in times of adversity a little can go a long way and an occasional celebration sweetens the days of hardship. There was little wherewith to rejoice, but complaint was at a minimum. Morale was good and the people did not dream of peace at any price. Their suffering only served to augment their perseverance, making them more determined to resist, instead of weakening their wills and shaking their faith in the wisdom of their course of behavior. The man in the street generally did exude a rabid, implacable hostility toward the enemy. Rather, he tended to accept the facts passively, going about his daily business as usual, taking what life offered and entertaining the belief that one day victory would ensue and he would lead a more satisfactory existence.

14. Crisis

It is now time to consider the general political situation during the middle of 1944. The huge, sprawling Japanese empire, which in less than six months from the outbreak of the Pacific War was extended to cover Eastern Asia and half the Pacific, was still intact and bore an imposing appearance. Only a number of islands on the fringe in the Pacific had been recovered. The Americans called the capture of these outposts, one after the other, "island-hopping." The newspapers of the day gave harrowing accounts of the battles between the Americans and the Japanese; they fought like barbarians and engaged in personal combat. The Japanese snipers were tied to trees so that they couldn't escape, and entire garrisons perished because they would not be taken captive. There was no general offensive in the area, as Roosevelt and Churchill had decided to annihilate Hitler first. In July 1944, General Tojo, the Japanese prime minister, resigned with his cabinet. He was widely regarded as the man responsible for the outbreak of the Pacific War and was bracketed by the Allies along with Hitler and Mussolini as the three chief malefactors of the world to be brought before a tribunal of justice when victory was achieved. His fall was hailed as a sign of the collapse of the Japanese military machine.

Affairs in Europe were going badly for the Axis. The tide of battle turned in Russia with the surrender of a German army at Stalingrad in 1943 after a frightful holocaust and the ruin of the city. The Russians then proceeded to drive the Nazis from the Ukraine and Crimea and, in May 1944, captured Sevastopol. By early August they were fighting on the outskirts of Warsaw. In November 1942, an army under Eisenhower landed in the French territories of Morocco and Algeria with the idea of eventually invading Italy from across the Mediterranean. After expelling the Italians and Germans from North Africa, the Allied forces attacked Sicily. In July 1943, Mussolini was overthrown and was kept as a prisoner by the person who ousted him, Badoglio. But he was rescued by his friend Hitler, who proceeded to defend Italy for him against the Allies. On June 5, 1944, Rome fell. The next day a great Anglo-American army of invasion crossed the English Channel to Northern France. The fate of Hitler was sealed, and the utter collapse of Germany was momentarily expected by a world a tiptoe for the announcement.

After securing the cities and ports in China, the Japanese armies had stayed practically bogged in the mud for years, unable to bring the war to a decisive conclusion. Under the shadow of the generally victorious stance of the Allies in 1944, the Japanese warlords became filled with desperation. It would be extremely difficult for them to get along once they were left alone to face the music. In a last effort to demonstrate their strength to their own duped people, whose morale was weakening, they launched a fresh and vigorous campaign from the Yangtze region southward. Their purpose was to cut a route through South China to Vietnam and Singapore to provide, if necessary, a land retreat for the armies in Southeast Asia. Evacuation by sea would not have been an option as the Japanese shipping fleet had been hopelessly wrecked.

Changsha in North Hunan had been a much combated area, and under a new onslaught it was captured. This was the beginning of the unexpected triumph that carried the foe across the provinces of Hunan, Kwangsi, and Kweichow up to the gates of Kweiyang, a triumph that was to prove as illusory as the chink of coins in a bankrupt's pocket.

Dating from 1942 a number of airplanes had been built in South China by Chinese and American engineers for purposes of counterattack. From them flew the bombers of the United States Fourteenth Air Force to disrupt enemy communications, destroy ground installations, and bomb enemy cities. The capture of these airfields was one of the principal Japanese objectives. They had been constructed with stupendous labor at tremendous speed, not with mechanical contrivances but with the patient, tireless hands of tens of thousands of laborers who quarried rock, leveled the areas, and paved the runways. To see them drag heavy rollers along the tracks, make excavations and embankments, and turn a barren waste in a few months into a center humming with activity made one realize the invincible spirit and boundless energy of the people.

With the ominous fall of Changsha on June 20, 1944, the inhabitants of Liuchow started making preparations for evacuating it. The first batch of the staff's families of our office left for Kweiyang. Though there was anxiety, there was no panic, and life continued almost as usual. While some people departed from Liuchow, more came into it from places nearer the front en route for the interior. Lodging houses did a roaring business and doubled and trebled their rents. Evacuees found it difficult to get transport on trains and trucks, which were crammed to capacity.

One of the saddest things was that in such a crisis some offices heartlessly chose to retrench their personnel, leaving them to fend for themselves. My office dismissed thirty-odd employees, including a good friend of mine, Kong Mun Sang, who had three children, one of them a baby six months old. He was a draftsman who had been with me in the Kweilin office, had been transferred to Liuchow, and had remained there with the change in the directorship of the office. He was considered expendable. Unable to find another job in Liuchow, he was forced to return to his native place of Canton. On the way his baby died of starvation.

One day I was surprised to find a hundred or so schoolboys evacuated by the government from Hunan staying in the vicinity of my office. They were about ten years old and were as unfortunate a crowd as could be found anywhere. They didn't cry, but they didn't smile either. They slept on the pavements and took their meals squatting in groups of four or five in the middle of a lane around a bowl of vegetable soup, the only accompaniment to their small bowls of dark-colored rice.

A group of students from Chung Shan University in Pengshek in Kwangtung fled to Liuchow, among whom were some originally of Hong Kong University. They wandered around the streets not knowing what to do. Their university had disbanded, and each student was seeking whatever sanctuary he could obtain through his own efforts. The Hong Kong students were experiencing what so many people in China had had to undergo—fleeing from one place to another more than once. Their way of life, and with it their appearance, had undergone a complete transformation. Vanished was the comfortable life they led in prewar days. In their new university they had barely gotten enough to eat. Instead of the well-dressed gentlemen they used to be, they now had the appearance of tramps. But I did not hear them utter a word of complaint, and they just carried on dully as a matter of course.

Even before Changsha was subjugated, the Japanese had advanced toward Hengyang. A strenuous contest for that city went on for weeks, and all kinds of rumors floated into Liuchow concerning its fate. Now it was said to have been captured; now the enemy was in retreat. In a newspaper called the *Liuchow News*, I culled the following report made on August 8: In the course of forty-seven days since June 23 when the war for Hengyang commenced, the Japanese lost twenty thousand men. For a long time they were unable to make any headway. Having brought up strong reinforcements, and with the aid of scores of planes, they bombarded and routed the heroic Chinese forces on the evening of August 4. There were heavy casualties on both sides. On the morning of the seventh, after most of the Chinese soldiers in the northern suburbs had perished, the enemy entered the city through that gap. Street fighting was in progress. The National Military Council issued a bulletin on the tenth stating that the street fighting lasted from the morning of the seventh to the next morning, after which the situation in the city was not clear. We understood that the place was lost.

The Japanese then pushed in the direction of Kweilin and took to the indiscriminate bombing of Liuchow, evacuation from which was accelerated. One night, they bombed a lane in which was located the hostel where I had dwelt for a year before. I had moved out shortly before that incident. A bomb crashed through the front part of the roof of the flimsy building, killing one man and injuring two women. The dead man was occupying the room just above the one in which I had lived. The place where I was staying then was not far away, and as I lay in bed I heard the bombing that sounded terribly close.

Troops were quartered in every empty building all over the town, and they slept on the floors of markets. By the middle of September, many shop fronts were closed, and the crowds in the streets, which had been much swollen with refugees, were considerably thinner. Even the newspapers had removed most of their equipment. The sheets were smaller and the items scantier and mainly concerned with the approach of the enemy. Purchasers grabbed whatever goods remained to sell. It was quite characteristic of human taste that the greatest increase and decrease in prices appertained to cigarettes and books, respectively. A packet of cigarettes more than doubled in price while a book sold for less than half of what it was previously. I noticed the same phenomenon in Hong Kong after its fall; most commodities quadrupled in price, but cigarettes quintupled, while books were sold at ten cents a kati.

I experienced once again the desperation and dislocation of war. Air raids became fiercer and more frequent every day. Unpleasant sights added to the confusion. I saw gendarmes round up persons of no occupation and tie them to one another with ropes; they were being forcibly pressed into the army. Corpses of men in uniform lay on the pavements, having perished from starvation or disease. The medical services had taken their departure, and cholera and dysentery were prevalent. A tremendous swarm of flies infested the town.

By early October the personnel of my office, who had been evacuated in batches, had all departed except for twenty-two men, including me, who were left behind to carry on the work until the last moment. We could not be said to be overjoyed at the prospect, for not only was the situation fraught with peril, but to save space in the vehicle left behind for our evacuation, we had sent away in advance those of our belongings that we did not need at the time, including our winter clothing. Should we by some chance still be in the place when winter was on us, we would have to endure the cold in addition to our other troubles. We were, of course, in no position to buy any clothes even if they were still available.

In the last days of my stay in Liuchow I had, strictly speaking, little to do, so I spent much time reading voraciously the books that I could purchase cheaply by the armful. Not taking into account its value as the nutriment of the mind, a book is the best of beverages. I also roamed through the streets to witness the progressive death of the city. The population had dwindled to a fraction of what it was; nearly all the shops were boarded up and goods were obtainable practically only from roadside stalls. The desolation of the town hit me like a thunderbolt.

The army erected barbed-wire barricades in the streets, while at the crossroads it put up circular concrete pillboxes. There were not many troops about, but the compound of our office was never free of them, one band after another arriving and departing. It was said that Japanese soldiers in plain clothes had infiltrated the city. Believing that they were their special targets, American servicemen didn't stay out late. Air raids occurred intermittently, and the rainy weather helped to make them less frequent.

During the first days of November, the armored columns of the foe surrounded Kweilin. Simultaneously the forces advancing up the Si Kiang, taking one ill-defended town after another, were fast approaching Liuchow. When they were a score of miles away, the last remnants of the population fled. The airfield was systematically destroyed, the eighth in order of the lost air bases. Thick sheets of roaring flame and exploding ammunition contrived to produce an inferno, mutilating runways and revetments and reducing warehouses and hostels to ashes. The teeming town that had been gradually emptied was now breathing its last breath. If it had not been for the earlier evacuation of the major part of the inhabitants, the mob now fleeing pell-mell would have bred incalculable confusion. Vehicles were piled high with baggage on which every inch of space was occupied by people who even sat on the roofs of the trucks, closely wrapped in their coats, with the cold winds driving against their faces.

15. An Inland Journey

At 8:00 AM on November 4, 1944, I left Liuchow and headed for Kweiyang, 631 kilometers away. There were twenty-two of our staff, including eight coolies. We crowded into an office truck that had been utilized for conveying stone, earth, and other materials to the airfield. The driver privately took in a family of six persons with an immense quantity of luggage and pocketed the enormous sum paid. There were also four of his friends. What with soldiers getting free rides, there were altogether more than forty people squeezed into a wretched space on top of a mound of baggage of diverse descriptions. Our driver complained of fatigue, for he had been sitting up late the last two nights and had lost ten thousand dollars at cards. It was popularly said that this was the epoch for drivers, as they were among the richest men in the land.

We set out on our journey under a cold, gloomy sky. I recalled with a number of inward curses the time more than two years previously when I had quitted Hong Kong under similarly inauspicious circumstances. For the second time, the dark sun constituted the cause—the sun, when it was rapidly climbing to its zenith, diffused poisonous rays of destruction, and now, when it was obviously declining, it could still display some of its baleful energy. But the conditions of departure were different. Hong Kong was suddenly attacked and was quickly surrounded in such a manner that the inhabitants were trapped and they left after its occupation, the city being a teeming hive when it succumbed. The terrors of the new misrule were experienced prior to departure. On the other hand, the present South China campaign was a process covering months. Each city knew beforehand the course of the Japanese advance. Before the arrival of the enemy, it was thoroughly stripped of its population and stood an empty hulk. A deathly silence enveloped each doomed town. There could be no jubilation for the victors, who entered a scene of stark desolation and were greeted by nothing but mute walls.

Our truck crawled along the solitary road at an average speed of twenty kilometers an hour while rain steadily descended the whole day and night. We passed Tatang and came to Ishan, which was thronged with people. Matsheds consisting of walls of straw matting on bamboo frames and roofs of thatch had been hastily erected to serve as dwellings and shops. We stopped for a couple of hours for lunch and thence proceeded more slowly, as the vehicle broke down for short periods now and then. With the rain pouring down in torrents, we arrived at Chinchengchiang at 7:30 PM when it was pitch dark. After taking our dinner, we passed the night in the truck, as no lodging houses had any space left, and rain trickled through the roof put up over the vehicle before its journey.

In spite of the discomfort, we fell asleep. I awoke at dawn to find the rain still exercising its prowess. There were numerous trucks in this place of a couple of miry streets and grass huts. We again started on our journey, and at 10:00 AM we reached Hochih, rain falling all the way. Hochih, a district town about 220 kilometers from Liuchow, had as far as I could see only one road of gravel and sand. There were two-story houses with tiled roofs and wooden walls but no electric lights. This place was to be the termination of the first stage of our journey. Eighteen of us occupied two rooms in a so-called lodging house where there was no service of any sort, and the only furnishings were beds made out of benches with planks resting on top of them. Our rooms were upstairs while downstairs in an open hall other lodgers slept on beds placed against one another. Most of our staff, who had been evacuated one or two months earlier, were still here, for no vehicles were available. The U.S. servicemen who had quitted Liuchow dwelled in an encampment in a field on the outskirts of the town. Parked beside canvas tents were jeeps and trucks. They had blown up the airfield on the seventh before their departure, the Japanese being quite near at the time. So went into ruin the last of the recently constructed airfields from which had flown hundreds of bombers.

I took walks into the countryside and observed the green hills and greener fields. I leaned over a goodly culvert and beheld a comparatively limpid stream. Occasionally, a crow sent its melancholy caw through the air or a solitary frog crouching in the grass on the edge of the stream hopped into view. In the evenings I watched the Milky Way, termed the

River of Heaven, a broad, irregular, cloudy band traversing the sky from one end to the other amid a multitude of stars of enamoring beauty.

On the twelfth, we resumed our journey and a few hours later arrived at Nantan, which was bigger than those towns passed hitherto, for it boasted more than one crowded street, and several banks were discernible. I found accommodation in a loft from which the staircase led straight to the space outside the front door of the house. The next day we were on the move again, but after traveling only a short distance, our vehicle broke down. One man was dispatched to catch up with the other truck belonging to our office and bring it back to tow ours. We waited in vain for its arrival, and when night fell, we slept in the vehicle cramped in the most uneasy postures. The night was dark and, to protect us from wild beasts and wilder brigands, we engaged two peasants from the nearest village more than a couple of kilometers away to come and take guard, but they could muster only one gun between them. We kept a fire burning by poking in pieces of wood. I retired at midnight when a drizzle commenced falling.

Morning broke with the hills swathed in mist and the sun quite invisible. Our messenger returned with the news that he had been unable to overtake the other truck. There was no alternative now other than to have our vehicle repaired on the spot, the driver going to Hochih to get the requisite materials. We moved into lodgings in the village, where in a matshed that sold food, we found straw-covered beds.

We dwelled for four days in the village that, containing about forty-five huts on either side of the highway, lived isolated from the outside world, before our antediluvian contraption was able to stir itself. After covering not more than a score of kilometers, it broke down again and we had to spend the night in another much larger village. There were numerous soldiers stopping here en route to the interior. We left the next day, and luckily the truck managed to keep moving for the whole of the twenty-five kilometers to a small town called Luchai, which was better than any I had passed hitherto. We halted for lunch, during which I met a couple of friends from Hong Kong, and we had a happy reunion. We exchanged accounts of our experience in China and, though their lives like mine had not been the pleasantest, they did not evince the slightest regret for having left their homes.

After capturing Liuchow, which they attacked from the rear, the enemy continued their advance, taking Ishan and badly bombing Chinchengchiang through which we had recently passed. It was said that they were proceeding toward Kweiyang from Hunan and were only one hundred kilometers away from it.

Shortly after departing from Luchai, we crossed the border into Kweichow, an arch marking the boundary and informing the traveler that he was entering another province, and then stopped for the night at a village, as our conveyance needed repairs. By the roadside, I saw two young girls vending tea and glutinous rice soup. They had been clerical workers of the Canton-Hankow Railway Department, which had rendered them no assistance but had left them to fend for themselves. After they left Liuchow, they maintained themselves as hawkers. Their utensils comprised a stove, two pots, six bowls, six spoons, and some cups, while they had borrowed four benches and a stool from some of the villagers to ply their trade. They looked cheerful enough in spite of their predicament.

Our truck required extensive repairs, and we spent two nights in the village before we made our departure in another vehicle dispatched by our office. It traveled at a speed of about thirty kilometers an hour and broke down thrice but, fortunately, for brief periods only. We reached Tushan, a sprawling town where a new airfield was under construction. We arrived at dusk and, as it was difficult and troublesome to find lodgings, I passed a sleepless night in the truck. The next day we came to Tuyun, a district town where I found accommodation in a lodging house that resembled a lodging house; that is to say, it had rooms, bedding, and attendants. For the first time on our journey, I enjoyed the luxury of a room all to myself.

The next day we came to Machangping at noon and, after repairs to the truck, left at 5:00 PM. Soon darkness fell, but Venus and a half moon shone in the sky. Cold and hungry, we arrived at Kweiting at 8:00 PM, and after arduous exertions I secured a bed.

Taking our departure from the very small town of Kweiting the next day at 9:00 AM, we finally arrived at Kweiyang, which, pending further developments, was our journey's end. What a journey! It took us 20 days to traverse 631 kilometers. Dirt, rain, cold, misery, a crowded, ramshackle vehicle, danger from brigands—these had constituted our experience. A truck journey was an affair of colossal discomfort, for every vehicle was crammed to considerably more than its full capacity, traveled with exasperating slowness, and broke down constantly. We frequently saw stalled trucks by the roadside. The worst was when the decrepit conveyance chose to cease its half-hearted functions when dusk was falling fast in a desolate region far from any town. The passengers had to pass the night within its narrow confines or sit around a fire of wood or grass. The situation was aggravated if the sky was pitch-black and a drizzle was in progress. It was not so depressing if the moon shone brightly, girdled with a golden aureole.

The road had grown increasingly rugged as we proceeded on our way, the land being more mountainous. The Southwest Highway, which we had been traversing, was a narrow road of water-bound macadam. From the nature of the terrain it had been difficult to construct. It presented steep gradients and violent curves. We had passed through numerous villages, mere collections of thatched huts, smothered in a somnolence hard to disturb. The towns were of inconsiderable size, but their populations had been swollen with the influx of refugees, and the housing problem was acute. Lodging houses were choked, and flimsy matsheds had been put up for use as dwellings and restaurants. The inhabitants were in a state of excitement, apprehensive of the apparently worsening course of the war. The countryside had left in me an impression chiefly of brown hills and short grass, as this ancient land had been stripped of forests.

Kweiyang, into which we made our way through one of its gates, was still standing though weather-beaten by the ages. It was a city of fair size, the capital of a province, which consisted of a lofty plateau with mountains enclosing pockets of plains whereon rested the towns. A popular statement had it that not a single li of land was level. The weather was very rainy with few days of sunshine. As in Kweilin, the city contained two main roads that formed an intersection at its center, where stood a clock whose four faces pointed toward the north, south, east, and west gates. Contrast always engenders a heightened sense of appreciation; it brightens the eye of attention. To one fresh from the heavy desolation of a stricken town, the city seemed to throb with life and gaiety. Life there was in plenty, but a potent current of uneasy feeling pervaded the atmosphere. It is disquieting to reflect that towns, which should be the peaceable abodes of industry and mutual exchange of benefits, are often the scenes of bloody carnage. Kweichow was a poor, undeveloped province, and its capital, which possessed no distinctive significance, served as a halfway house for travelers into the interior, one road leading in a northerly direction to Chungking and another going westward to Kunming.

There was a park in the town named Chung Shan Park. All the parks that I visited in various towns bore this appellation. This particular one was small and contained few trees, the principal feature being a pool of green water, in one corner of which was a red pavilion connected to the brink by an ornamental bridge. In a cage were two varicolored fowls with lengthy tails, members of two varieties found near Kweiyang, called the "golden fowl" and the "wild fowl."

To return to the war, the Japanese continued to press forward. Their marauding cavalry proceeded farther into the hinterland, going forward rapidly by trotting along bypaths rather than the main highway. It came to within eighty miles of Kweiyang where, outdoing its strength, it was brought to an abrupt halt on encountering the best Chinese troops, some of whom had been withdrawn from the northwest and others who had been victors in Burma. The threat to Chungking and Kunming was eliminated. Immediately thereafter the initiative was wrested from the hands of the aggressors, who were steadily compelled to retreat. By the next June, Liuchow was reoccupied, and Nanning—not far from the border of Tongking, lost during the same period of Japanese victories—was also retaken. The invaders were pushed back to the coast, and their projected rail communication with Southeast Asia was irretrievably severed. Their present South China campaign amounted to no more than a brief raid of little, if any, advantage to them.

16. Loping

I had expected to stay in Kweiyang for some considerable time but, as it turned out, I was there for only five days. The director of our Liuchow office had secured a new job—namely, the construction of an airfield in Loping, a town in Yunnan near its boundary with Kweichow. With the loss of the air bases in Kwangsi and Hunan, new ones were to be built farther in the interior. I was selected to go with the advance party to perform the survey work.

The road from Kweiyang led to Kunming, a distance of 664 kilometers, but it was even more rugged than the highway from Liuchow. At certain sections, and not short either, it zigzagged up and down mountains in a series of continuous loops. From its narrow surface hacked out of the rock, one peered down on the valleys below, where rivers ran and where cultivated fields were occasionally visible. From a distance the road through the mountain passes looked terrifying and impossible to negotiate with its sharp bends and steep grades, but when one was on it the feeling vanished. Villages were widely separated and farms meager. There was little traffic, and it appeared improbable that it would ever witness much.

Our party of nineteen persons left Kweiyang on November 29. As no trucks were permitted by the government to proceed into the interior, we made use of nine horse carts that were capable of accommodating six persons each. A cart was drawn by a sturdy, carefully trained pony, which trotted along slowly but with unfaltering step. There was one consolation in that, unlike the mechanical vehicles, the carts didn't break down, and though progress was slow, at least they kept moving. The temperature became colder, and the day after we left Kweiyang it was 48° F. Passing through villages and sleeping at night in small towns, we arrived at Anshun where we had to wait for trucks. When I awoke the next morning, I found the roofs of the houses covered with snow. Anshun was a fairly large town with the streets paved with square blocks of stone. Our lodging house was a four-story stone building with each room containing two or three beds. To keep warm, fires were made of charcoal burning in braziers resting on wooden stands.

On our journey it was quite common for us to come across aborigines called Miaos. They differed little from the Chinese of the Han race in physical appearance. Were it not for their peculiar, striking dress I would probably not have noticed them as being different from the other peasants. They kept to their primitive customs, spoke their own language, and lived in villages, cultivating the land.

After staying in Anshun for five days, our vehicles arrived and we took our departure early in the morning. We stopped for lunch at a village called Huangkuoshu, less than a hundred miles from Kweiyang. Here we saw the celebrated waterfall, the greatest in the land, 215 feet high. The white water catapulted into a green river. During the summer rains, the cataract grew torrential and the leaping waters, silvery sheets of cloudy spray, filled the village nestling peacefully by their side with their majestic symphonies.

At other times, they murmured their secrets in soft, aerial song. In such manner did nature register its protest against discordant war. Wordsworth had reason to lament, "What man has made of man."

After passing through Annam, a district town where we were accommodated in a guesthouse (a reasonably good one kept by the China Travel Service), we came to the village of Shatzeling where we turned off the highway to Kunming and wended southward to Loping. The stretch of road after leaving Annam was the worst imaginable, traversing in zigzag fashion along the sides of mountains higher than those previously encountered. Often we were swathed in mist and could discern little in front of us. Villages were few and far between. Our conveyance, which mercifully did not collapse, crawled along at ten kilometers an hour.

After Hsingjen we passed through a larger extent of flat land than had saluted our eyes for many a day. The villages were better looking, and throughout the entire length of the highway on either side were farms interspersed with buildings. We reached Hsingi, from where the road to Loping had been out of repair for a long time. So we set forth westward in a train of sedans and horses on a journey of about one hundred kilometers in very cold weather. The type of conveyance we had, known as a huakan, was used for hilly country and resembled a litter or palanquin in which one could stretch oneself almost at full length. It was light and consisted of a bamboo frame borne on the shoulders of two men. Bedding was spread on it, and a sheet of cloth suspended across the top as an awning. We traversed a mere footpath alongside the hills with the keen wind blowing in our faces. We spent the night in an inn, where horses were stabled in the courtyard, in a miserable village on the border of Kweichow and Yunnan.

The next day we resumed our journey, our path going through even more mountainous country. We then came to Panchiao, a small town, after which we traveled along a motor road on level terrain until noon on December 12, when we arrived at our destination.

Loping, more than a hundred miles to the east of Kunming, was listed as the administrative town of a district, but it was indistinguishable from a village, consisting of a single narrow street of irregular blocks of stone, juxtaposed any which way and roughly rammed together, and a row of houses on either side. But it contained the yamen of a magistrate. It was a real backwater with not a single modern utility visible—there was no electricity or piped water—nor for that matter any ordinary facilities. No amusement of any known species was available, and life was as hard as the claws of a crab. The people were as poor as poor could be. They had no winter clothing, and for warmth each person carried a small basket with a pot of burning charcoal. For the peasants existed a severe round of unremitting toil from the first glimmering of dawn to the last glow of twilight. Every six days a fair was held in the solitary street, which was then lined with hawkers and packed with humanity, becoming quite different from its normally deserted appearance. It lasted for one day from early morning to nightfall. The principal commodities were baskets, crockery, firewood, charcoal, straw mats, blocks of salt, needles, old clothing, rice, vegetables, and fruit, such as tangerines, pears, and persimmons.

The war had never made its ogreish appearance in this place peacefully hidden amid the hills. No death-dealing bombers visited it to rain destruction and terror. Beneath its cool summer skies and thick curtain of winter fog it pursued its serene existence. When one thinks of war in connection with the middle nation, it is extremely erroneous to imagine that all the people were equally affected. This was far from being the case, as in this extensive territory only a comparatively small section did witness actual warfare. If a battle raged in one corner, others were at peace. Until they stood on the brink of it, the ordinary people pursued their vocations and spun out their lives in curious apathy.

The airfield that we were going to construct was located five kilometers to the south of the town beside a highway. On one side ran a river and on the other jutted hills. It was winter at the time we arrived, and when I went out with the surveying party I found the work site, a field, enveloped in thick fog and the grass converted into masses of pure white pearls of frost. The plants were festooned with sprays of seemingly snowy flowers. The earth was hardened, cracked, and covered with ice, and the mountains in the distance gleamed brightly with snow.

After about a month in the town, we established our office in a large village about two kilometers from the airfield. The surrounding countryside with its farms and uncultivated land presented an attractive sight. Our office was housed in a new, tolerably fine building, the biggest in the district. The owner of the mansion took eight years to build it, and he continued to reside in one wing. He was originally a horse driver, but it was said that by engaging in the illicit opium trade he had become wealthy. He was now the local magnate, held the post of commandant of the district militia, and was quite a character with his eight wives and thirty-odd children. He was in his forties at that time, was hefty in build, possessed an imposing appearance, and though not exactly fierce, was certainly not soft. His reputation was none too good, and I wondered whether he was secretly in league with brigands. Once, I saw an American officer smoking opium at his place. He had great influence with the district magistrate. He was at loggerheads with a Chinese interpreter working with the American army, and he persuaded the magistrate to arrest him and put him in prison on some trumped-up charge; however, with the help of his American employers, the interpreter was released and, to forestall further trouble, he left the district soon afterward.

In Loping I came to be acquainted with some officers and men of the United States Air Force. As the airfield was constructed with the aid and for the use of the Americans, we had right from the start a resident engineer who had his office at the site. He was Captain Klika, who was of Hungarian origin and who had served in China for one year. He expected the war to be over soon so that he could return home and sleep, as he put it. I used to go to his office on business, and I took the opportunity to borrow from him a considerable number of publications intended for the perusal of their servicemen. These books included poetry, fiction, and other forms of literature. In Loping there were no bookshops, and I would have been hard put to get reading material otherwise. Among his staff I came to like Sergeant Klaiber and Corporal Hill. The former was in his middle thirties at the time but his hair had turned gray. One day I showed him a pamphlet that I had written while in Kweilin about the fall of Hong Kong. He said it was very good and offered to get it published in the States. Apparently his credential for getting it into print was that he knew an author living on the same street as him in his home town. Nothing, however, transpired beyond the one conversation I had with him about the book when he returned it to me. Corporal Hill was much younger than Klaiber and, like nearly all Americans whom I encountered in China at the time, he scarcely ever smiled—I presume the strain of serving in a war-torn country amid strange people with incomprehensible ways was not exactly mirth-provoking. I understood from him that he had made some invention.

As the airfield progressed and was put to use, more and more American servicemen arrived until there were several hundred of them quartered at the place. There were even Chinese Americans among them. To the local people who had never seen them previously, the Americans were a queer lot in their physical appearance as well as their ways. Because of the exigencies of the war, they were allies and were therefore tolerated, but there was no particular liking for them. Their wealth was not something to attract admiration, and they tended to be arrogant rather than friendly. The Americans, on the other hand, entertained a low opinion of the Chinese although they might not say so openly. One trait about them was their obsession with sex. They were apt to talk about it in season and out of season. In the land of China they found themselves sex-starved, as they called it, but the Chinese had no sympathy for their predicament.

A nasty incident occurred in Loping. One evening the director of our office invited some American officers to dinner. There were about a score at the table, including hosts and guests. While the dinner was in progress and the guests were quite merry, one of our engineers came to me to say that three American servicemen had arrived at the village in a truck and, holding pistols in their hands, had seized a girl, the wife of one of our laborers, while she was standing in front of our office. They had forcibly dragged her into the vehicle and driven off to the stunned surprise of the small crowd around. I informed the officer who was the commander of the Loping air base, and he immediately dispatched an assistant to investigate. It transpired that the soldiers had taken the girl to the airfield, and two of them raped her. They then released her and told her to go home. While stumbling about crying in the dark, she was found by the search party. The three soldiers were apprehended and sent to Kunming for court-martial, and the two rapists were sentenced to life imprisonment. The Americans whom I met were shamefaced about the incident as well as surprised at the severity of the punishment. One or two expressed their opinion that the drastic sentence would very likely be reduced after a time.

I liked to take walks around the countryside, treading the paths through the rice fields. There were ponds covered with beautiful lotus blossoms and streams with willows drooping over them. It was pleasant to rest beneath the shade of a pine tree and gaze at the majestic mountains in the distance or sit in a bamboo grove and watch the magpies flitting nearby. In winter when it snowed I spent hours watching the flakes falling down lightly—pure, white, like cotton wool. How beautiful the sight could be! Earth and sky blended into a monochromatic scene.

The villages, however, were far from agreeable. They were filthy and the lanes, just sheets of red mud covering irregular blocks of stone, were never swept. The only cleansing performed was by rain, which streamed in torrents toward the fields. The thatched huts of diverse sizes and in varying degrees of dilapidation sat huddled together. They were constructed of rough timber, the posts and beams of logs of pine, the walls of bamboo coated with lime plaster, the roofs of grass from the nearby hills, and the floors of beaten earth. Lofts made of planks might be erected near the roofs and were used for sleeping or for storing grain. The only openings in the walls were doors, windows being considered superfluous. The interiors were gloomy even in daytime, while at night little oil lamps shed a modicum of glimmering light. The furniture consisted of a rough table and a few stools.

The villagers led an extremely bleak life; they were nobody's business save as sources of taxation, and they possessed no facilities of any description. Water for drinking or cooking was transported from none-too-salubrious ponds in wooden buckets dangling from shoulder-poles. They wore ragged cotton clothing, and their food consisted of maize or rice with some vegetables—and even these were insufficient. In winter, when it could be very cold, they sat shivering around small braziers in which burned a few lumps of glimmering charcoal. To them toil, endless toil in the fields, from earliest dawn to vanishing twilight, was the order of the day. It is in the nature of ants to work the way they do, but for human beings to enact a similar routine over their food supply is not matter for lyrical ecstasy. They enjoyed no recreation whatsoever, and they passed their lives amid grain and inanities, thoroughly ignorant of the outside world. Their bodies were broken and their minds stunted. Life was so hard that one wondered how they could tolerate it. In fact, they made no complaints, as they had never known anything else. It is quite common nowadays to hear publicists, trade unionists, and workers say that adverse economic conditions drive the people to desperation and revolution. This is not necessarily the case. People become dissatisfied with their conditions and clamor for change only if they have known better ones, or there are thinkers and revolutionaries to show them the possibility of another way of life.

Looking at these villages made me realize keenly the undesirability of all villages. The village is a relic from prehistoric antiquity, and the sooner it is abolished the better, for it cannot be properly developed to give its denizens an adequate degree of civilized life, a life with easy access to cultural activities and surrounded by a satisfactory material environment. It is uneconomical to furnish a small community with the latest conveniences. A village need not necessarily be squalid, but even the best cannot provide an adequate range of amenities. The town is the proper abode of every person, the model town being of modest dimensions and well developed. There is nothing to prevent the farmers from living in a small town, going out to their fields in the morning, and returning to their homes in the evening.

In our office, we had hardly any recreation. Our principal diversion was an infrequent feast held for various reasons—for example, to celebrate the Spring Festival, to bid farewell to a group of colleagues departing to another place, or on the occasion of a marriage when the persons invited bestowed gifts of money sufficient to pay their share. Some people were given to playing Chinese chess or checkers and some to mahjong. Our main holiday, but quite an unofficial one, occurred during the lunar New Year when we were off duty for three days. We held an uproarious feast on New Year's Eve while snow mantled the ground outside. We felt carefree and forgot that we were sequestered in a remote village in a war-torn, poverty-stricken land. The beauty of want is that it takes so little to make for merriment. Working hours were long, commencing at 7:00 AM. We went to bed early, mainly because dim oil lamps were not conducive to wakefulness. I used to expound to some colleagues my views on diverse matters relating to religion, philosophy, political and economic organization, language, and civilization in general. We held lengthy discussions that we enjoyed. In the cozy days at Hong Kong University, my friends were not so receptive to new ideas or so interested in the serious problems of life and civilization.

In an office such as ours employing hundreds of people, there were all types of characters. They came from all provinces. A particular friend of mine, named Teng Mu Hsi, hailed from the North. He was interested in business and endeavored to save some money from his meager salary to utilize as capital. He was an engineer, but he did not think of becoming a contractor as so many other engineers did for the purpose of acquiring wealth. Instead, he toyed with the idea of being a merchant or manufacturer. He was instrumental in inducing a few colleagues to join him in setting up a restaurant that also sold groceries. After the war, he started a cigarette factory in Liuchow, but it came to an untimely end.

There was Lin Chi Min from Chekiang Province. He was one of the very few persons I knew who talked in favor of communism. The people in my office did not normally discuss politics, and if any were enrolled members of the Kuomintang, they did not disclose it. From their conversation one would have thought that they were not interested in political matters, but their apparent apathy was probably due to discretion. Like most folk in all countries they outwardly acquiesced to the government or the ideology of the day. Lin Chi Min did not like the Kuomintang, but his grumblings against it and advocacy of its rival probably signified nothing more than letting off steam. I sometimes wonder what became of him under the Communist regime and whether he was satisfied that his wish had come to pass.

In our office there were female employees, only a few and mostly the wives of male members of the staff. Women were not segregated from male company, but it was not the fashion for the sexes to mix freely. It was seldom that a man ever conversed with a woman. Many of the men were not married. With their exiguous earnings they felt no desire to burden themselves with families, but that did not make them go running after girls. Scandals were unknown, and the sexual urges and aberrations of the permissive age were not problems with them. The advanced view never exploded in their brains, a view probably also held by prehistoric peoples, that sex is a glorious need.

The construction of the airfield went on apace, and the runway, together with the main works, was in full operation by the end of April. A continually increasing number of planes of the United States Air Transport Command arrived. By early June the project, including all the installations, was completed. Thenceforward, we had little work to do and were only waiting to return to Liuchow, which was expected to be retaken from the Japanese at any moment.

17. Kunming

The province of Yunnan is a vast, high plateau crossed by mountain ranges. Continuous with the arid Tibetan Plateau, it is cut by a great number of narrow valleys, which are fertile and bear crops of rice and maize. A curious phenomenon is that many villages have to be reared at an inconvenient height, a thousand feet maybe, above the cultivated tracts. The Si Kiang, about 1,600 miles long and one of the greatest rivers in China, has its origin in this plateau, from which three rivers of Southeast Asia also take their rise: namely, the Red River of Vietnam, the Mekong of Thailand, and the Salween of Burma. Rainfall is abundant mostly in summer. The province contains rich mineral deposits of tin and copper.

In its eastern part sits its beautiful capital, Kunming, with incomparable scenic splendors. Situated a mile above sea level, the city enjoys an equable climate, the rare blessing of a perennial spring, bathed by the sun and brushed by gentle breezes. While in Loping, I went to Kunming twice by plane and, when I left Loping for good, it was to Kunming that I first went and this time it was by train. The aircraft that I traveled in was an American military transport plane, which had collapsible leather benches along either side and could accommodate twenty-four persons. It took off from the airfield that we constructed and landed in Kunming on the outskirts fifty minutes later.

The history of Kunming is ancient, covering a span of more than two thousand years. In its checkered career it commenced as an independent kingdom before the Han Dynasty, degenerated into a district town, and finally emerged as a provincial capital in 1919. The slow process was undertaken of transforming its medieval aspect. But it was the war that radically affected its character, raising it from its conservative somnolence, bred of isolation, into a center of jostling activity. Migrants from the teeming ports, fleeing from barbaric insolence, swelled its population—never before did it hear so many dialects. When the only route into Free China was Burma Road, it increased its strategic importance. The receiving end, a position it retained when all land communication was lost and supplies could enter only over the Himalayas, transported in a continual succession of planes.

The changes wrought by the prolonged War of Resistance, as the Chinese called the Sino-Japanese War, were far-reaching in their effects. There were many factories of diverse types and sizes, their plants having been transported from their former sites, and farmers learned to be skilled artisans. Educational institutions were likewise transplanted. The Southwest Associated University, an amalgamation of three universities formerly in Peiping and Tientsin, was originally set up for the benefit of the students who studied in them before and who, choosing to leave their homes, traveled inland, chiefly on foot, via Changsha in Hunan.

The social effects of the migration were beneficial, tending to break down provincialism and build up patriotism. In normal times, the inhabitant of a district would scarcely venture to move elsewhere, for he would have found life in another province unpalatable from the unsympathetic attitude of its original denizens. Now, he was welcomed and his ways tolerated with understanding. The differences of dialect have tended to be exaggerated by many Western writers. In truth, they have never been the formidable barriers alleged. Save for Fukien and Kwangtung, whose dialects are more peculiar, the various provinces speak variants of Mandarin with mutual intelligibility. When the inhabitants of different parts of the country were brought into close proximity, they learned to understand one another very quickly and the standardization of language was promoted.

The city blew with the wind of life. It was far from the actual theater of war, though now and then there appeared a threat, as when the enemy was advancing into Burma or rushing toward Kweiyang. In its shops the sale of the noted products of the province went on uninterrupted. It was also the market for goods which in the main it did not itself produce. Articles made of ivory imported from Burma were to be found in profusion, ranging from seals and chopsticks to curios of intricate craftsmanship. Dainty ornaments of enamel, amber, and jade made their gleaming display in the center of the city. However, the prices of such commodities were erratic, especially due to rampant inflation, and it required know-how to distinguish between the genuine and the spurious and to drive good bargains. Articles, such as cigarette cases and crockery made of fine tin from the mines of Koukiu, about 150 miles away, were popular. The famous marble-producing center of Tali to the west enabled the city to supply a wide range of marble products. Yunnan had its special varieties of ham, mushrooms, and tea that were exported abroad.

Kunming was quite a fine city with concrete buildings and asphalt roads. Good business premises were everywhere, and there were cinemas showing first-run pictures from Hollywood. Restaurants were plentiful, serving diverse types of cuisine—the Peking, Shanghai, Canton, Szechuan, and Yunnan styles and even the Western. After experiencing a succession of small towns and villages with their medieval conditions and living in cities subject to air raids, I was surprised to find a city so far in the interior existing in apparent peace and having some semblance of modernity. Life was unhurried. There were crowds in the streets but they were not uncomfortably dense. The principal landmarks were the permanent arches of the Golden Horse and the Jade-Green Cock. These splendid structures had been erected to pay homage to two celebrated mountains deemed the tutelary guardians of Yunnan. Legend had it that a golden horse galloped over from India and was captured on the mountain bearing its name by a prince who became ruler of the land. As for the jade-green cock, it was a phoenix said to have been seen long ago flying about the other mountain by the ancestors of the Yunnanese.

During the War of Resistance, Kunming was the main communicating center between Free China and the outside world. It was connected by an air service with Chungking. Domestically, highways were speedily built with a minimum of tools and an immense output of human energy. Local roads already in existence were connected, and lanes for use by horses, sedan chairs, and pedestrians were widened and improved, thereby making them accessible by motor vehicle from the provinces of Kweichow and Szechuan.

Kunming abounded with scenic delights. It is not easy to do justice to the beauty of the glamorous Kunming Lake, a spacious expanse of limpid, blue water, over which waved bamboos and cypresses. How delightful it was to cruise there in a sampan in the evenings, inhaling the balmy air permeated with the fragrance of blossoms, which grew the whole year round—not only sailing within the lake but up a small river which flowed into it! The lake was so much admired that an artificial "Kunming Lake" was made at the Summer Palace of the Manchus in Peking. Beside the lake, which was located on the western outskirts of the city, lay Ta Kuan

Park with the Three Arches monument standing in stony majesty at its entrance. The park, which was named after its main pavilion, contained a library, a zoological garden, and a swimming pool. When I visited it, part of the land was submerged by heavy rains and the buildings sat like guardians of the place.

On the western side of this great lake was the equally celebrated Western Hill, which, viewed at a distance in sunny weather, shone like copper. It was entrancing to spend a day tramping about it and sitting by its meandering streams. Its dense growth of perennially green trees was set against a background of red earth. One could walk along roads up it to several temples, crowded with strange miniature images of clay. There was a path with nearly a thousand steps of stone. On the edge of a cliff overhanging the lake was a structure called the Dragon Gate from which one enjoyed through the transparent atmosphere a panoramic view of the city and the surrounding country. It was a favorite spot for the local picnickers, who could travel to the place by boat or car.

Within the city in the northeastern corner was Yuen Tung Park, located on a hill and containing fine trees, flowering plants, and picturesque cliffs and rocks. Set in a lotus pond at the foot of the hill reposed a monastery, the biggest in the province, said to have been in existence for about twelve centuries. South of this hill and a short distance away was another hill, Wu Hua Shan, on and around which stood the provincial government and municipal offices, public buildings, museums, art galleries, temples, and parks in a picturesque array. To the west of it this hill overlooked Green Lake Park, with its red roses and redder camellias. Lotus flowers grew in profusion in this lake, their perfume wafting on the cool breezes. Myriads of captivating fishes filled a pond beside a pavilion where the townsfolk spent their leisure hours munching groundnuts and washing them down with green tea. Day and night people strolled in the park, away from the din of the city.

In the region around Kunming were other places of interest. Five miles from the Small East Gate on the top of a hill was the remarkable Brass Tiled Temple built in the sixteenth century. Its pillars and tiles were of brass, while the balustrades were of carved marble. The Black Dragon Pool was on another hill ten miles from the northeast corner of the city. Said to be seventy feet deep, it was protected by railings of stone; one gazed entranced into its limpid depths and at the beautiful fish swimming in it. Considerably farther away from the city to the southeast was the Hot Spring, noted for its misty scenery and the siliceous nature of its water.

Bathers were loud in their praise of its tonic properties. Still farther away was the Stone Forest in Lunan, with its rocks of strange shapes and cliffs of weird forms, the upright pillars dwarfing the trees in their height and grandeur. The scene was entrancing, especially when it was bathed in sunlight and the blue sky above was flecked with white clouds.

Kunming has left a profound impression on my mind and has remained my most treasured memory of China. Its natural beauty alone would probably not suffice to account for this indelible impression. But contrasted with the squalor, air raids, makeshift buildings, primitive conditions, and other unfavorable aspects of the numerous towns and villages that I had encountered, it probably appeared to me more wonderful than it really was. The worth that we place on anything is normally conditioned by the extent of the ease or difficulty of its availability. Rarity magnifies the image of value; people would not prize diamonds the way they do if these were as common as pebbles on the seashore.

The happy days I spent in Kunming were marred by an incident that I propose to relate, as it was the only event of its kind—civil strife resembling civil war—which I witnessed in China. It was really of a seriocomic nature. I have to go ahead of my story a bit, as the incident occurred after the end of the Sino-Japanese War

I was on my last visit to Kunming where I arrived on September 26, 1945. I was staying in a large, traditional type of mansion in the center of the city. The brick building was surrounded by a lofty wall, which shut out all sight of the street as well as its cacophony and which enclosed a garden glowing with magnolias and chrysanthemums and alive with fluttering white pigeons. Life was peaceful, and I was enjoying myself roaming around the town or visiting scenic spots. The war had come to an end, I felt free and easy, and I thought I was well rid of even the alarm of hostilities. On October 3, I woke up early in the morning to hear the sound of gunfire. I lay in bed thinking. What might this portend? The guns continued their spasmodic chatter. I got up and found all the residents of the house talking in subdued tones. On inquiry I was told that fighting had broken out in the city and a curfew was on. What fighting? Surely the Japanese couldn't have suddenly revoked their surrender and landed parachute troops in Kunming! As they were of an irrational breed and had done the strangest things before, this phenomenon was not exactly possible only in the realms of fantasy. No one knew what was actually the matter, and we were completely mystified.

What had actually happened was an unexpected, ridiculous scrap between the provincial and the central government forces. A little drama, more in the nature of a comic opera, involving the change of governorship of the province, was unfolding. Lung Yun, governor of Yunnan for more than ten years, was being forcibly relieved of his post and ostensibly promoted to the barren job of president of the Military Advisory Council, a national organ. His successor was Lu Han. The Kunming Garrison headquarters and gendarmerie headquarters were being abolished and replaced by the central government Defense headquarters, which was responsible for the curfew. The displaced governor was inundated by a wave of distress about his removal, for he apparently looked on the province as his private property. Fearing trouble in the interval of change of government, the Defense headquarters had posted soldiers all over the town. There was some slight fighting between the local and the central government troops.

We were not aware of this story until later. In the course of that day rifle, machine-gun, and even cannon fire burst out at irregular intervals. Because of the curfew, we had to depend on the scanty store of rice left in the house, and we had to make do with rice gruel for dinner. In the evening, however, the electric lights came on and the Kunming Broadcasting Station aired its program as usual. The next day the curfew was lifted at 10:30 AM, but for some time to come it was in force every night from 8:00 PM to 6:00 AM. On October 5, T. V. Soong, the brother-in-law of Chiang Kai-shek, and General Ho Ying-ching came to Kunming to invite (a euphemistic way of saying "to force") the ex-governor to accompany them to Chungking. On the morrow, Lung Yun left Kunming and the troubles vanished. He had been a loyal supporter of the central government for the entire duration of the War of Resistance, and he was now liquidated. On October 7, the curfew, which had been in effect not only at night but for some hours in the daytime throughout the period, was completely removed and the city returned to its normal appearance. The tempest in a teapot was over.

18. War's End

We must now go back and trace the course of events in the world. Toward the end of August 1944 when the populace of Paris heard the cannon of the American forces thundering in the suburbs, they revolted and, in cooperation with the French Forces of the Interior, delivered the city after heavy street fighting. The Vichy government fell to the guerillas, and France was cleared of the Nazis. In the early days of September, the Allied forces crossed the borders of Belgium and Holland. They were soon in the Rhineland and in March 1945 advanced toward the Elbe. As for the Russians, in the last few months of 1944, they advanced through Romania and across the Balkans. In January 1945, they captured Warsaw after a protracted siege. They entered East Prussia and raced toward Berlin, which they reached on April 20. On April 30, a couple of days after Mussolini was shot by Italian partisans, Hitler committed suicide in the underground bunker where he had been living. Germany surrendered on May 7, and the Third Reich, which was intended to last a thousand years, screamed into extinction.

The ferocious war in Europe was over. But in the East, though the prospect was vastly lightened, strenuous work yet remained to be accomplished. In China, the jubilation over the collapse of the Nazis was brief and not unduly exuberant, seeing that, so far as it was concerned, the end of the colossal conflict was still to come. The struggle did not relax. Speculation was rife concerning the further span of time needed to crush the Japanese, whose doom was sealed. The world expert made the habitually inexpert prophecy that two years were necessary. It is extremely dubious whether history and political knowledge could ever be made scientific enough to allow the accurate prediction of near or distantly future events. Along with exact knowledge of existing circumstances and valid inference, such factors as new developments, unexpected occurrences and a hundred imponderables too often cause the political prediction to resemble metaphorically a cat that has failed to catch its rat.

Nobody expected the islanders to collapse so dramatically within a bare three months. Their empire still possessed a majestic appearance. The only reclaimed territories of any extent were the Philippines and Burma, and even these were not completely cleared of their presence. Their land forces had not been shown to be weak. In reality, their seemingly solid empire was hollow within. Years of unnatural strain, the universal detestation produced among the recalcitrant populations by the oppressive rule of rampant troops, the mutilation of their navy and air force, the wrecked cities in the homeland with consequent dislocation of industry— all these made their superficial strength a sham. They were on the verge of a precipitate downfall.

In October 1944, U.S. forces landed in the Philippines, and in February 1945 Manila was captured. The war was brought to Japan itself when planes continually pounded Tokyo and other industrial cities with ever-increasing activity. On August 8, the U.S.S.R. declared war on Japan. The Japanese were now fighting alone against the whole world. Even the Germans in both world wars never stood at any time absolutely without allies, though these might have been of no real help.

The Japanese at first refused to accept the Potsdam Declaration calling for unconditional surrender. On August 6, the most ferocious weapon of war yet invented made its cataclysmic entry when the first atomic bomb fell on Hiroshima, raining total destruction. A thrill of excitement, incredulity, and horror shot through the hearts of men. A second one unloosed over Nagasaki three days later brought the war to an end. The Chinese War of Resistance, the Pacific War, and the Second World War terminated on August 14, 1945, a memorable day. Japan had attained the unique distinction of being the only country in the world ever to capitulate on the strength of air raids. Its empire was extinguished like an array of candles blown out by the wind.

It might be as well to pass a few remarks on the atomic bomb. Those dropped on Japan were not formidable compared to the hydrogen bombs developed since then. The Japanese succumbed so easily principally because they were completely taken by surprise at the effects of a new weapon. It is doubtful whether a determined people nowadays would surrender if nuclear bombs were dropped on its territory. Furthermore, now that this device is not confined to one country, its use would only lead to mutual destruction. The conscience of the world would not excuse its employment whatever the circumstances might be. However, in spite of everything, some country might still resort to it in a moment of madness. It is ironic to think that the Second World War with all its horrors should have terminated and peace and joy restored with the greatest horror of them all.

After the fall of Liuchow, the Japanese had pushed into Kweichow Province in the closing months of 1944 and thereafter proceeded no further. But the situation was precarious. More territory in southern China had been lost and most of the newly constructed airfields captured. More railway lines had come into the hands of the enemy, who now had control of the entire length of the Peking-Canton Railway.

It was all the more demoralizing in that in the latter part of 1944 and the first months of 1945, the Allies were victorious in all the other theaters of war. One of these was Burma, from which Chinese troops along with the American and the British were expelling the Japanese in an inexorable manner. A new land route between China and the outside world was under construction. The explanation lay in the increasing economic plight of the country, as evidenced by the galloping inflation. The Nationalist armies were badly equipped and on the verge of starvation. The aid rendered by the United States was little—some air support and a thin stream of material resources. The Nationalist government had been in the war against Japan much longer than the Americans and even before their entry was already on the defensive, locked in a poor, undeveloped mountainous region.

When Germany fell, the Chinese were undoubtedly happy but not particularly elated. China was fighting Japan before the conflagration in Europe began with the Nazi invasion of Poland, and it looked as though it would be at war an indefinite time longer. Neither were the American GIs in China exactly jumping with merriment, for they were not going home immediately.

We were all still in the war and had work to do. Liuchow was recovered at the end of June, and the staff of my office was returning there to rebuild the airfield. But as we hadn't enough transport, we had to depart in batches. From the first group to reach it, we learned that the population was scanty and the houses had largely been burned down.

Then came the capitulation of Japan. I was still in Loping. We were all agog with excitement as news of the momentous events rolled in day after day in rapid succession. The atomic bomb was something we had never heard of and it rocked our understanding with wonder and bewilderment.

It was incredible, diabolical. We speculated whether the reports concerning its destructive power were true, for at first we were given to believe that each bomb obliterated an entire city from the face of the earth. One person remarked that it was immoral for war to be conducted in this horrible manner, while another wanted to know what was wrong about it and stated that the ferocious Japanese only got what they deserved. It was by no means certain that the fanatical enemy would surrender, and we vaguely wondered what would happen if it didn't. However, as it turned out, the Japanese were not prepared to face portentous terrors that had never entered their calculations. When the news of their capitulation was received, my friends and I were in the midst of a discussion on diverse topics. We stopped to listen to the radio and, after the first expressions of jubilation, we resumed our conversation.

"I shall return to Peiping," said Teng Mu Hsi. "I left it in 1937 and have been wandering about from one place to another. I wish I were home."

"It is going to take some time before we can return to our homes," remarked Lin Chi Min. "There are millions of us in the interior, and where are we going to get the transport? According to a statement of the central government, it will put into operation fifty airplanes, twenty-nine steamers, and four thousand trucks, which can carry a total of eighty thousand men monthly. If that is all the transport available, many people are going to wait a long time. In Chungking itself half the two million inhabitants are refugees."

"That is a problem," chimed in Hu Yao Hsien. "My home is in Hankow. However, when the worst comes to the worst, I suppose I shall walk."

We all laughed. We had not laughed for quite a long time.

"You must be a wonderful walker," said Chi Min quizzically. "I envy your prowess."

"I suppose you'll be returning to Malaya," said Mu Hsi, turning to me. "It will take time before you can get a ship."

"Yes," I replied. "I presume our office will be wound up. I wonder whether we'll disperse from here. It's going to be difficult for me to get my own transport from this place to the coastal region."

"I don't think we'll disperse from here," said Wei Chih Yu, a native of Tientsin and the only married man in the group. "We were originally supposed to return to Liuchow but, though there is now no need to restore the airfield, we'll probably be going all the same since our office still exists in that place, which is nearer the coast. Our director is not likely to retire for good. He will try to secure some other engineering job and, pending the outcome, will hold the staff together in Liuchow."

His forecast turned out to be correct.

"We had better go to Liuchow first before going home," said Mu Hsi. "Easier that way."

We all nodded our heads in agreement.

"All our lives we have been troubled and maltreated by the Japanese. I hope we are rid of them for good!" remarked Chi Min.

"I don't suppose they'll rise up again," said Yao Hsien, "but there is nothing certain in politics."

"If the Germans could recover to wage a second world war, why couldn't the Japanese become strong and aggressive again?" remarked Chih Yu. "It doesn't look as if the Allies want them to remain weak forever. According to the Potsdam Declaration they are to be free to decide their ultimate form of government. Could they change their nature? Why shouldn't they later want to revive militarism?" he asked rhetorically.

"You evidently have no liking for them," laughed Mu Hsi.

"Like them?" shouted Chih Yu. "I might as well like tigers and wolves! I suppose you adore them!" He was evidently hugely angry.

"Come now," said Yao Hsien placatingly. "Don't shout! Mu Hsi was just trying to be humorous. I don't suppose any of us esteems them. If we did, we wouldn't be here. Let us hope they have learned a good lesson and won't become marauders again."

I listened to the rain falling steadily outside. Although it was August it was not at all hot. In fact, the weather had been quite cool and it had been raining most of the time for some days past.

"It's lucky that the war has come to an end sooner than most people predicted," I remarked. "How would you like it to continue for another two years, say?"

"What the inflation would be like by that time I shiver to think," said Mu Hsi, pulling a long face.

"The war has lasted long enough," stated Chih Yu. "It isn't interesting to be in the position of the man who leaves his native village young and returns home old and nobody recognizes him. What a nuisance that is!"

"You know," said Yao Hsien, "two years ago I thought the war might drag on for a long, long time and might even come to no definite conclusion. I am glad it's over."

Just then Mrs. Wei Chih Yu came to ask her husband to go and buy some eggs and cooking oil, for she had run out of them.

"I suppose, Mrs. Wei," said Mu Hsi, "you are packing up to return to Tientsin."

"You get me an airplane and then I can start making ready!" she replied with a giggle.

"You ask Mr. Chen here to get you one," said Mu Hsi jocosely. "He may persuade the Americans to give you a seat. He is their good friend, you know!"

We all laughed and our gathering broke up.

V-J Day, the day when Japan signed its formal surrender, was September 2. In the official celebrations spanning three days in every town in China, items included 101 bursts of thunderous mirth resounding from cannons and shrieks of joy lasting for ten minutes issuing from the throats of air-raid sirens proclaiming the "All Clear" signal. Crackers burst in showers, eloquent meetings were held, and processions wound their triumphal way along the streets. Defeat before victory sweetens victory. The Japanese forces throughout their far-flung captured territories laid down their arms separately in different areas and waited in dejection for repatriation to their homeland. Defeat after victory embitters defeat.

Thus terminated the Second World War, the most stupendous struggle in history. The last of the Axis countries ended its military dream. A nation of aggressors, blinded by uninterrupted triumph for half a century, had now traveled to a sorry denouement. There was a time when it evoked admiration for its achievement in rapid emergence from medievalism, when voices were uplifted in praise of its land of cherry blossoms, its energy, and patriotism, its apparent capacity for progress. But it chose instead to pursue the will-o'-the-wisp of martial dominion, fraught with peril to others and of no genuine value to itself. Its religion was developed into a buttress of false patriotism, its emperor worship became a symbol of racial arrogance, its industry was geared to military adventure, and its outlook was a negation of the rights of man. In its downfall is embedded a lesson—the folly and evil of militarism. The capital of aggression earns the interest of destruction.

It is well to make an attempt to appraise the Japanese and reflect over their aspirations as they were at that period of their history. One feature of their onslaughts, as of those of the Germans, was the swiftness of their victories, acquired by long, intense preparation and seizure of the opportune moment. But after a certain stage was reached they stayed bogged in the mud, unable to proceed any further. In the China War, after the fall of Hankow and Canton, spectacular gains eluded them.

After a long time they did achieve momentary success in the South China campaign of 1944, but this was no more than the last act of a desperado, who knew he was doomed and was seeking a way of escape.

In the Pacific War, their series of triumphs culminated with the fall of the Philippines, Burma, and several other islands, after which they began to experience slow but steady defeats. How the Japanese ever expected eventually to emerge victorious against the United Nations with their extensive territories, vast populations, incomparably greater resources, and a stronger determination, born of consciousness of right, was known only to them.

Their ephemeral glory bore resemblance to a bad dream. Ancient Greece as a state endured only a short span of time, but it left behind a legacy second to none. The invisible power wielded by its thinkers and artists is greater than that of any dictator, to say nothing of being far nobler and more beneficial. That it could do so was due to its intellectual preeminence and the supreme originality of its mind, which enabled it to make discoveries unknown before its age. These monuments of its genius could never perish; they are endowed with a unique life. Japan made no contributions to world progress and did no good whatsoever. It only longed for evil and deserved its defeat. From the end of the shogunate it forged ahead to become a great power, solely on the strength of its arms, without enriching by one tittle the store of human knowledge. Essentially reactionary in outlook, it attempted to breathe life into the fossils of feudalism. It displayed the pettiness of its outlook in its lack of originality, obtuse neglect of the true good, and absorption in militarism. Its military prowess, were it unquestioned, would still be no sign of intelligence, for in history barbarians were very often tremendous conquerors. It is in peace that we find the more glorious fields of human endeavor, requiring a higher display of genius. The mind of Plato outshone that of Alexander, and Hitler was an imbecile compared to Einstein. If the world were never to advance, then reactionary tendencies may elicit praise. But if the sublimest truth and the greatest good is progress, then such attitudes should be categorically condemned and their advocates relegated to the realm of contempt.

19. Return Journey

On September 18, 1945, I left Loping for good together with the remaining personnel of our office. It was a fine, sunny day with a blue sky bedecked with shards and masses of white, luminous clouds. Combined with the green fields and the red earth, the scene constituted a bewitching color scheme. We went by truck to Kutsing, a small town with a railway station. We stayed there for about a week when we took a train for Kunming, where I witnessed the incident of the change of governorship previously described.

Inflation had been blithely engaged in scaling Mount Everest. Just before the Japanese surrender rice cost in terms of the Chinese National currency $250 a kati and gold $240,000 a tael. The general price level was five thousand times what it was prewar. Ironically, with victory came the bankruptcy of bankers and merchants. Gold and cloth dropped to half price, and hoarders unloaded their goods at a loss. The government appeared concerned about this and made loans to the businessmen to maintain prices at a high level and save them from ruin. Prices dropped continually to about the middle of September when they started rising again.

On October 25, I took my departure from Kunming on my way back to Kweiyang, which I reached four days later. The countryside and the villages and towns traversed had not suffered any particular ravages on account of the war. On the road were many trucks carrying soldiers on the way to Nanking. I wondered vaguely how many of them had their homes in that city or its vicinity and what sort of welcome awaited them from their families and friends.

Kweiyang was no different from what it was when I last saw it, save that the spirit of tension was now absent. On the journey back to Liuchow I retraced the same route, passing through the same places. Tushan, 230 kilometers from Kweiyang, had been thoroughly gutted before the arrival of the Japanese, but by now it had been partially reconstructed. The enemy had pushed a short distance beyond this town on the road to Kweiyang before their progress was arrested. As the journey continued, the villages and towns encountered looked bare and desolate, for the invasion had caused them to be reduced to heaps of rubble and gaunt, blackened walls and pillars. A few buildings had been repaired and matsheds hastily erected. Along the highway, all the bridges and culverts had been demolished, and temporary timber structures now spanned the rivers, big and small.

I reached Liuchow on November 6, almost exactly a year after I had evacuated it. Thoroughly destroyed as a result of the attack by the enemy in 1944, it had been considerably restored in the course of the few months since its recapture. Bare walls stood here and there, but new wooden buildings were numerous and the town did not look much different from its former self. But the central, erstwhile most important section north of the river still lay in a state of complete havoc. The pontoon bridge had not been put back, and boats were needed to cross the river. Electricity was not yet available.

The town presented a busy scene. A good proportion of the crowds was composed of sojourners en route for their homes, as everybody was anxious to return to his long-deserted native place. According to the proverb, "to stay a thousand days at home is good; to be away for one day is distressing." Transport had not diminished its exorbitant charges, and it was about as difficult to look for as the proverbial needle in a haystack. The reluctant sojourners were likely to take a long time indeed before they set foot in their villages.

A few days after my arrival in Liuchow the postal service was resumed, and I hastened to send letters to my home in Malaya and friends in Hong Kong. The service was so unreliable that what I dispatched to Malaya failed to be delivered. But my brother, Cheng Or, had been informed of my whereabouts by a friend of ours, Fong Wahl Hun, who had returned to Hong Kong from China. He forwarded through him a letter to me. This, received in late December, was the first communication I had from Malaya since 1941.

Our office, which had been reestablished when the first batch of our staff set foot in Liuchow after its recovery, was housed in a new group of buildings. These were located at the south end of the airfield, which could still be utilized by only a few China National Aviation Corporation planes, for the Americans had relinquished it and left Liuchow. I lived in one of these office hostels, occupying a room with three other persons. The members of the staff had hardly any work to do, but they had been retained and were still drawing their salaries pending the outcome of the director's securing a new job in some place when they would follow him there. As for me, my intention was to return to Hong Kong and thence Malaya, but I had to abide for some time longer owing to the difficulty of securing transport not only from Liuchow to Hong Kong but from Hong Kong to Malaya.

As soon as the war thundered to its close, the race began between the Nationalists and the Communists to gain possession of the territories being delivered up by the Japanese. I have referred little to the Communists hitherto, but it would not be out of place to present a brief account of their history here.

The Chinese Communist Party came into existence in the early 1920s and was at first in league with the Kuomintang to subdue the warlords and unify the country. The Kuomintang under Sun Yat-sen was at that time leftist and welcomed Russian cooperation. After the death of Sun Yat-sen, Chiang Kai-shek in command of the forces of the Kuomintang led them to victory in 1926, the country being thoroughly antipathetic toward warlords and civil war. But Chiang Kai-shek veered toward the right while the Communist elements attempted to capture Shanghai and other cities. The Communists were worsted in the struggle, and Chiang Kai-shek practically unified the country in 1928 when his forces entered Peking in triumph.

The Communists were, however, far from being eliminated. They instituted a Soviet type of regime in a mountainous tract of land in Kiangsi where Mao Tse-tung now came to the forefront. The Nationalists sent armed expeditions to destroy the regime and finally dislodged them from their stronghold. In 1934 the Communists withdrew from Kiangsi and made the "Long March" of six thousand miles to Shensi in the northwest where they established new headquarters at Yenan, living in caves in the loess hills surrounding this small town. They escaped annihilation at the hands of the relentless Nationalist forces in pursuit of them on account of the mountainous terrain that they traversed.

After the subjugation of the warlords and the ostensible unification of the country, Chiang Kai-shek had to face two menaces, internally from the Communists and externally from the Japanese militarists. At that time, the Japanese threat was more serious and Manchuria was occupied in 1931. The chauvinists clearly showed their intentions when, after the acquisition of Manchuria, they got a firm grip on Inner Mongolia and moved into Northeast China. They wanted the whole country. Chiang Kai-shek, however, considered it more important to eradicate the Communists first before fighting the Japanese, and the way he yielded to the aggressors was the beginning of his decline in popularity among the people.

Chang Hsueh-liang in Sian was supposed to be battling against the Communists in the northwest, but his susceptible mind made him listen to their plea of patriotism that Chinese should not fight Chinese but should combine to resist the Japanese invaders. When Chiang Kai-shek visited Sian in December 1936, he was detained by Chang Hsueh-liang, and the upshot was that he came to an agreement with the Communists to stop their civil war. The Japanese began their general invasion in July 1937.

Throughout the eight years of the Sino-Japanese War, the Nationalists and the Communists maintained their truce. They did not resort to any internecine warfare on a significant scale, but there was no genuine cooperation between them, for they could never trust one another. Naturally, the Nationalists bore the brunt of the war against Japan. Territory lost was under their jurisdiction, while the Communists only occupied a small, inaccessible corner of the country. While the Nationalists were getting more and more exhausted with the prolonged war, the Communists were conserving their strength. They scarcely ever fought a pitched battle of any extent against the enemy. They might, of course, have been in no position to do so. They confined themselves to guerilla activities and inflicted considerable damage on the enemy, but this type of warfare has hardly shown itself effective in expelling a foreign invader. At best, if sufficiently prolonged, it helps to demoralize, weary, or waste the substance of the foe. They extended the territory under their control and increased the strength of their army. Their party had a membership of 100,000 at the commencement of the war and 1,200,000 at the end of it. In 1945, they had a compact organization and a hardened army.

It is doubtful that two parties with such dissimilar ideologies could ever really cooperate, especially when they were dictatorships. Both were intolerant toward other parties and, though both were fundamentally patriotic, they were more concerned with their own power. In the presence of their common enemy they could stifle suicidal warfare, but their alliance was uneasy with no positive results and to all appearance was temporary in character.

At first the two parties made half-hearted attempts to come together. The Communists even declared that they recognized the Kuomintang as the legitimate government of the country and that they would dissolve their own government and army. In the People's Political Council with only advisory powers, the Communist and other parties as well as the Kuomintang had representatives. Soon, however, relations grew strained. The Communists never abolished their government and army. In fact, they ran their territory like a sovereign state. The Nationalists not only blockaded the northwest region, but an army of theirs even attacked and defeated a Communist army in 1941 and put it out of action.

Again in 1944 the two parties in the face of the Japanese victories endeavored to effect a reconciliation. The American government, more concerned with the prosecution of the war against Japan, also intervened to bring them together. But no positive results materialized, as mutual distrust was too strong to overcome. Even the U.S.S.R. appeared to support the idea of a rapprochement between the two parties and professed to believe, like America, that the Communists were not genuinely such. The main protagonists in the drama, however, had made up their minds and were not disposed to listen to the advice of the foreigners.

In China under Nationalist rule Communism was outlawed and it was not referred to openly. Among the people I knew there were few who professed any sympathy for it. It was seldom discussed even in private, so it was difficult to know what people really thought. Ostensibly, most persons regarded it as a nuisance and an impediment to national unity but not as the future successful supplanter of the Kuomintang. They did not see much to admire in the Nationalist government, but that did not make them yearn for Communist rule. They grumbled at their hard life but blamed it on the war.

When hostilities came to an end, the main problem confronting the Allies was the reoccupation of the territories to be returned by the Japanese. The governments that formerly owned the lands were, ipso facto, the ones to receive them back. Within a short time the previous owners repossessed their various territories. In some countries there were Nationalist movements to oust the colonial powers, but we need not refer to them here. In China, however, trouble rose right from the start, for there were two claimants. As the government recognized by the world to be the legitimate government of the country and as the former authority in control of the lost lands, the

Kuomintang automatically assumed that it had a prior right to them. But the Communists were in no mood to accept the claim. They surreptitiously moved into whatever areas in North China they could secure, and they infiltrated the rural areas of Manchuria. The Kuomintang secured most of the territories, but it was inept in the tasks of reconstruction. Relations between the two hostile parties grew from bad to worse, and civil war broke out in Manchuria in April 1946. Incompetence, corruption, internal dissension, and the disillusionment of the war-weary civilians and soldiers alike led to the military debacle of the Nationalist government and the establishment of the People's Republic of China in 1949.

At the time that I was in Ludlow in the closing months of 1945, the impending civil war between the Kuomintang and the Communist Party was apparent. Everybody in our office was unhappy about this, for everybody was sick of war. On a day in December when a group of us were sitting around a fire, the conversation turned to the political situation in the country.

"We have had eight years of full-scale war against the Japanese, but we bore it without a murmur because we were buoyed up by the thought of the prosperous peace to come," remarked Chang Wen Yen. "Now it looks as though we are going to have another war."

"This land never seems to be free from war, which would appear to have become endemic," I said. "From the period of the warlord to the Japanese aggressions, there has been no real peace."

"We are born in an unlucky era," stated Teng Mu Hsi lugubriously.

"Properly speaking, war has never been completely absent from any country," remarked Chien Chi Hsiung, "but few countries have it so persistently for decades. It is an unenviable distinction."

"These Communists are a pestilence," said Kang Yun Yao angrily. "Don't they have the sense to realize what they are doing to the country?"

"They think they will provide a better government," responded Hu Yao Hsien. "The present government is corrupt."

"Every warlord thought he was going to make a good government," asserted Yun Yao just as belligerently. "We are sick of professions of good intentions."

"After all, the Kuomintang hasn't brought greatness, prosperity, or peace to the country," said Chi Hsiung.

"How was the government going to do all that with warlords, Communists, and Japanese doing their utmost to wreck the country?" asked Yun Yao dramatically. "I am surprised that it did anything at all!"

"What has it done?" asked Yao Hsien dryly.

"China is one of the five great powers," said Yun Yao.

"In name," remarked Yao Hsien shortly.

"Whether in name or in reality it is a source of pride," chimed in Mu Hsi. "Besides, I don't see why the United Nations should accord it the status of a great power if it were nothing of the sort. At least, they must think that it will soon be one in actual fact."

"What is the use of being a great power when people are poor and hungry?" demanded Chi Hsiung. "I prefer to have a good salary."

"You are having one now, aren't you?" remarked Wen Yen banteringly. "Your salary is, if I am not mistaken, about fifty thousand dollars a month. A few hundred dollars either way make no difference."

"What was your salary before the war if you were working then?" I remarked casually as I stirred the firewood in the hearth.

"One hundred dollars," replied Wen Yen.

"And you could live on that much better than you are living now," stated Chi Hsiung. "I wonder whether civil war will break out."

"There have already been skirmishes," said Wen Yen. "The way I see it, the war will develop and be quite serious."

"I suppose it will last many years," remarked Mu Hsi. "Who will win?"

"There is no question of that," responded Yun Yao with conviction. "The Communists will eventually be destroyed. The only trouble is the country will not be having the peace, which it should be having right away."

"I hope your confidence is not misplaced," said Chi Hsiung.

"Whoever wins later, we are in for trouble now," remarked Wen Yen. "I think it will be a long war. The country will be in greater ruin than it is now."

"The papers say that General George C. Marshall is coming as an ambassador to reconcile the two parties so that they work together for the good of the country. Do you think he will succeed?" asked Mu Hsi.

"Unlikely," I said. "The two parties have been enemies, secretly or openly, for twenty years, have very different policies, and are both out to control the country. They will never be able to cooperate for long."

"Quite right," responded Mu Hsi. "This is not the first time the Americans have intervened. Last year Vice President Wallace and later General Hurley came for the same purpose. They failed in their attempts."

20. Hong Kong Again

On December 28, 1945, I started on my return journey to Hong Kong, it being a pretty cold morning when I took my departure from Liuchow. I had for company a couple of friends from my office, one going back to Shanghai via Hong Kong and the other to his home in the New Territories. The truck in which we traveled accommodated twenty-five persons sitting in three rows on bedding and luggage. It was closed at the back and had gratings by the sides and an entrance behind the driver's seat. It traveled at an average speed of thirty kilometers an hour but, refreshingly dissimilar from the other vehicles that I had experienced, did not break down at all. The route ran through a cultivated plain with many villages and sizable towns. We settled for the night at Kweihsien, which looked better than Liuchow.

The next day it was quite sunny. When we reached Yunghsien in the afternoon, we had to tarry for two nights there, as about eighty military vehicles were lined up to cross the nearby river and we had to wait our turn. In the course of the journey, at several river crossings a tug towed a raft with our truck on it to the opposite bank. The road along which we had been traveling was extremely dusty. After a day in the vehicle our clothing, hair, and faces were deep in red dust. On the last day of the year, we came to Wuchow after relinquishing the truck at a small town where the motor road terminated, and thence proceeding down a river in a sampan for about an hour.

Wuchow, situated on the border of Kwangsi at the junction where the Kwei Kiang joined the main river flowing from the direction of Kweilin, was important as a center for collecting the products of the region for transport to the coast. On the next day, when the inhabitants of the city were celebrating the official New Year by suspending flags from their windows and gazing at "lions" that danced their obstreperous way through the streets, we set sail down the Si Kiang to Canton. What we embarked on was a barge towed by a steamer and furnished with eighty beds arranged in two rows, one on either side down its entire length. However, there were so many people that passengers slept in the central passageway.

The Si Kiang, a broad river with green rippling water and lush banks, made a pleasant sight. Our boat stopped at a dozen towns, generally for a short while only. The monotony of the voyage was relieved by vendors of medicines and other wares, who came aboard at diverse places, each opening his campaign with a voluble oration or an amusing story. For a certain stage of the journey a blind girl sang Cantonese opera to the accompaniment of a squeaky fiddle played by her guardian. One of the most pathetic of all persons was a sightless songstress, not uncommon in the land, wandering about to earn her precarious livelihood. Food was sold on board, but many passengers had brought sausages, eggs, and other comestibles along and purchased only rice and vegetable soup to eat with them. We arrived at Canton at 11:00 PM on the third but, as rain was falling steadily and it would be difficult to get a lodging house, we waited until early the next morning to disembark.

I stayed in a hotel in Hopak, the major section of Canton north of the Pearl River. Thousands of small craft, including sampans, junks, motorboats, and launches, heaved at the waterfront. The river was spanned by a fine steel bridge. In contrast to the interior of China, the city looked modern with multistoried buildings, streetcars, clean, wide, asphalt roads, good shops, and neon lights. The streets were straight and level. At that time the population had been reduced to about 700,000, much less than before. Canton fell in 1938 and lay for seven years under the heel of the oppressor. It had suffered a severe conflagration and had been repeatedly bombed. However, it was said to look little different from what it was before.

There were about twenty thousand Japanese soldiers waiting to be repatriated, and they were spending their time usefully as road-sweepers. They still wore their uniforms, but their behavior had undergone a complete transformation. They stood in the vicinity of their quarters smiling and chatting instead of scowling. They were permitted to roam the city without guards. They no longer appeared bloated with vainglory and oozing with ferocity. They acted with seeming modesty and gentleness.

Canton was a historic town more than two thousand years old. Legend attributed its origin to five Immortals who came to its site riding through the air on five rams, which on their departure were metamorphosed into stone. Hence the city got its appellation of the City of Rams. It was known to Roman merchants, and from ancient times it had trade relations with the countries of Asia as far west as Syria and Arabia. Stretching back to the sixth century, Cantonese junks regularly sailed with cargoes to the lands of Southeast Asia. Its monasteries were of great age. The Monastery of Five Hundred Lohans situated in the suburb of Saikwan was founded in the year 503 but was rebuilt in 1855. Ranged along the sides of a big hall were figures of the five hundred lohans, or disciples of Buddha, among whom was, strangely enough, the Venetian Marco Polo, conspicuous for wearing a hat of alien type amid a multitude of shaven pates. The Six Banyan Monastery, built more than 1,400 years ago, had a superb pagoda about 235 feet high and possessed a rare collection of Buddhist relics.

Canton was a center of revolutionary activities in modern times and contained many monuments in honor of those who strove for the overthrow of the Manchu Dynasty. The Sun Yat-sen Monument, a worthy tribute to the founder of the republic, an impressive stone structure with a marble floor, was over two hundred feet high. It had a winding stone stairway of fifteen flights, each having about thirty steps. To render the climb less exhausting one could rest on seats of imitation marble beside the stairs.

The city had been well modernized in the two decades prior to the outbreak of the Sino-Japanese War. It had been deliberately transformed, its traditional aspects receding into the background. Narrow, tortuous lanes of granite gave place to broad thoroughfares of asphalt. The sedan chair yielded to the motorcar, and a bus service covered the entire city. New types of buildings arose—factories, banks, and hospitals. The city, which was initially confined to a site on the northern bank, gradually expanded until it sat astride the Pearl River, including several islands in it. Modern bridges, including the Pearl River Bridge, were built in the middle of the city connecting its two parts. Constructed of steel throughout, the Pearl River Bridge was six hundred feet long and its center span could be opened to afford passage to vessels sailing up and down the river. The ancient wall of goodly width and height, valuable enough when the town it enclosed was not likely to hear the roar of cannon, was destroyed to make room for roads where mechanical vehicles might race along. Through its picturesque gates, above which reposed captivating pavilions, had tramped generations of men. Its ruins, over which hung the romantic aroma of antiquity, became objects of curiosity. The harbor was reconstructed, a portion of the river straightened, and a new bund built. Wharfs and warehouses for the use of big ships were provided. Pearl Island, which was said to have come into existence at the site where a pearl fell into the river, became part of the mainland when the intervening channel was filled up with rock.

The commercial metropolis of South China, which also held a strategic position militarily, adopted with rapidity the new Western ways and inventions. The telephone and the radio made their appearance to the astonishment of the incredulous inhabitants, and oil lamps were ousted by electric bulbs. Spacious public parks blossoming in resplendent variety and containing pavilions with green roofs curling upward at the eaves were constructed. Modern buildings and offices came to alter the scene.

Industry developed apace, and chemicals, textiles, paper, glassware, metal tools, electrical supplies, bricks, matches, soap, household goods, and canned food were manufactured in great quantities in big factories. Nevertheless, the ancient handicrafts still prevailed. Fanciful work of jade, ivory, and silver, porcelain ware, articles of bamboo, blackwood furniture, painted fans, curios, and beautiful products of lacquer exhibited their abundance. But these gentle arts hid themselves in secluded streets away from the bustle and roar of roads of recent origin.

Though the war had ended only about five months ago and the city was returned after years of enemy occupation and neglect, it was a lively place with great crowds in the streets. Its busy teahouses betokened good business. Prices were cheaper than in Liuchow for most commodities, but room rents were higher and restaurants charged more for the same food. The picturesque junks and more efficient steamers sailed down the river with their cargoes. The floating population who lived in boats was much in evidence. The streets were congested with a hotchpotch of vehicles—motorcars, horse-drawn carriages, handcarts, bicycles, and rickshaws. The buses never seemed less than full. It was the middle of winter but the weather was mild. The people of Canton differed not at all from the people of Hong Kong in respect of dialect, appearance, manners, and way of life. The two cities therefore had a strong resemblance, except in the matter of the natural terrain, for the look of a town rests largely on its architecture and its inhabitants.

At 7:00 AM on January 6, I took my departure by the Kowloon-Canton Railway, which at that time was in a woeful state. The train, which left for Hong Kong only once a day, was not even certain and was crowded to overflowing capacity. The journey, which covered a distance of only ninety-odd miles, would have been quite comfortable if there had not been such a tremendous concourse of passengers, who not only filled every seat but sat in the passageways on their luggage or stood in cramped positions so that it was impossible even to move one's legs. I was not surprised when the guard found several passengers without tickets. In the congestion it was quite a feat for him to be able to undertake any checking at all. And the noise! The clatter of the vehicle was nothing compared to the vociferous din. Men and women chattered in loud voices, and their throats seemed made of metal to be able to produce such nonstop streams of sound. Children screamed and wailed as though for the fun of it. The passengers were of all sorts and ranks and were dressed in diverse garbs. The train rushed past pleasant fields and villages. The industrious farmers were bent over their paddy fields or vegetable gardens. Women in their black samfoos worked alongside them, even dragging ploughs. Children were exuberant as they rode on water buffalo. We arrived at the border town of Shumchun where the sinuous river of the same name formed the demarcation line between the New Territories and Kwangtung Province.

As the train steamed over the border into the New Territories in the afternoon, I gazed at the scene and vividly recalled old times. There was a rice field and a duck farm and, while murky, rugged hills with their steep slopes turned into cultivated land stretched into the distance. We passed Fanling and came to Taipo Market. From here to Taipo and onward to Shatin, the train skirted the coast, and I gazed entranced at the blue bays and inlets. Villages shot past with their brick houses reposing somnolently in the cold weather, and stone quarries covered with red earth revealed themselves. I could see Taimoshan, the highest mountain in this region—3,144 feet to be exact—which I had climbed previously. It was bare, sparsely covered with short grass. The train plunged into darkness in the tunnels and roared its way out again. I recalled cycling about Taipo with a friend and sitting alone by a cove at Shatin enjoying the peaceful scenery.

The train continued its journey and rolled through the middle of Kowloon. Residential houses flashed past, and business premises were alive with shoppers. The train eventually steamed into the railway station at the tip of the Kowloon Peninsula overlooking Victoria Harbor. I glanced at the clock tower—it was three thirty-five. I proceeded to Nathan Road and checked into a hotel for the time being.

Hong Kong wore an aspect not much different from what it displayed before the war. There stood ruins of bombed and gutted buildings, but the indestructible streets remained practically unscathed. The crowds were also considerably thinner, for the great exodus had reduced the population of

1941 to a third at the time of the reoccupation in 1945. Now the people were returning in ever-increasing numbers. But there were the same streets, the same buildings, and the same firms functioning in the same way. Save for the price level, which was higher by four or five times, one might imagine that life was being led under identical conditions.

The electric and water supply systems were as good as before. Buses and trams ran as of old, but somehow taxis had not yet resumed operation. The buildings of Hong Kong University were still intact but they were unoccupied and neglected. I felt it a bit odd that so little seemed altered after years of enemy occupation and desolate confusion. The same old things were restored with amazing speed. It was not only natural phenomena and scenic vistas that remained unchanged, but human works too were not altered to any considerable extent.

I met many friends, and nearly everybody I knew before was still alive looking little changed. None of them had achieved any remarkable success in life, and none had fallen into dire poverty. Among my friends almost the only difference I could find was that many of them had gotten married. I spent a lot of time wandering around the streets of Kowloon and Victoria by day as well as by night. It interested me to watch the human scene and to note the variations in the place from what it was prewar. Owing to the great decrease in population, it seemed to me that business activity was less hurried and life was lived at a more leisurely pace. The populace was tired after the traumatic experience of the occupation, and it went about dully, having no great expectations. At that time there were no signs of the tremendous burst of activity that was to come later and the huge influx of refugees that was to make it more unwholesomely congested than prewar. In fact, the change that was to ensue in the wake of the upheaval on the mainland was more momentous than that produced by the occupation, which had left no permanent effects, being merely an incident after whose passing the people just resumed their former mode of existence.

One day I was walking along the sidewalk of Nathan Road, the long, wide, level street traversing Kowloon in a north-south direction and constituting its spine. I was stopped by a friend who had been living in Hong Kong throughout the occupation. After preliminary greetings we adjourned to a nearby café.

"How did you fare during the occupation?" I asked.

"Pretty bad," he replied. "Little food and little of everything else. For lack of petrol, few buses were running."

"Why didn't you leave the place?"

"I had to take care of my family."

"Was the town peaceful?"

"The Allies came and dropped bombs, especially in the dockyard area. The Japanese were tyrannical but as time went on they became less violent, not out of kindness but because they knew they could not last for very long."

"Didn't you feel that the occupation would continue indefinitely?"

"No. Of course, from the newspapers one had a distorted view of the course of events, but people could learn the true state of affairs from the radio and from people who passed in and out of Hong Kong."

"It's a misfortune that we have had to undergo this nasty experience of war, isn't it?"

"Worse than nasty. It has destroyed my career. My university studies ended prematurely, and I wonder if I can resume them."

"What were you doing these few years?"

"I was serving as a shop assistant. I still am."

"We should be glad that at least we are still alive, sound in body and limb."

During the period of the occupation the port might be regarded as having no history. It led a pallid existence, the population decreasing, food growing scarcer, and prices getting higher. In a certain sense it lived in peace, as it saw no warfare save occasional air raids. Its destiny was settled in other theaters. It passed its life in the twilight, the twilight of dull misery, waiting for the dawn of liberation, which appeared to the inhabitants slow in making its appearance. An air of doom hung over the city, which did not suffer the death of destruction but which was in a state of lethargy.

The Japanese conquest of the small territory of nearly four hundred square miles was just a passing interlude in its history, an inconsequential episode. It resembled a bad dream. Why was it chosen to be among the few main targets of bombing by the aggressors when they suddenly unleashed their planned attacks in December 1941? Why was it assaulted on the same historic day as Pearl Harbor, Manila, and Singapore? Hong Kong had no great value militarily or territorially and, if it was to be invaded, it could have been done at leisure. Presumably it was selected because it was near the Japanese forces in China. It was an easy conquest and a prestigious blow to British imperialism. Furthermore, it should have been accorded the privilege of entering the Co-Prosperity Sphere as soon as possible.

After staying for a couple of days in Kowloon, I had removed to the island to reside with a friend, Cheung Wing In, who had a flat in Happy

Valley. I passed the days quietly—reading, seeing friends, wandering around the colony. Chinese New Year came and went, the people celebrating it as enthusiastically as ever. All shops were closed and most offices had a two-day holiday. I received letters from friends in Liuchow saying that their chief had secured a new job in Manchuria as director of a highway bureau and that they were waiting to go there. My aim was to get home to Malaya as early as possible, but there was a dearth of ships at the time and it was most difficult to get a passage. Later I found that the British Royal Air Force ran a service for the public, and I managed to secure a seat in one of their planes. I left Hong Kong in March after staying there for more than two months since my return.

I ascended the Peak, which towers over the island and surveys the scene below. I felt as relaxed as a bird in its nest. Over a smooth sheet sparkling like glass lay Lilliputian vessels at rest, while some craft glided softly in a slow reverie. The flat, gray roofs of Victoria reposed on either side of strips of road on which crawled trams and buses. Not a sound arose from the hubbub far below. From across the narrow stretch of water the promontory of Kowloon jutted with its blue hills, while inlets carved the sea with their delicious curves. The breezes blew languorously, whispering the awful secrets they had known. Crimson glided the great sphere of the sun down into the west to its slumber. What a beautiful scene, at which I had so often gazed in rapture! Conquerors come and go. Nature remains. What terrible events had this same sun witnessed. It rose and set, disdainful of the puny, ephemeral triumphs of man, his cruelties and vanities.

I took my departure from Hong Kong early the next morning. The plane was only a small one, and the passengers who had assembled at Kai Tak Airport numbered hardly a score. Our destination was Singapore, but the plane was to stop in Saigon and continue its journey the next day. The weather was auspicious and we were in good spirits. We entered the plane and made ourselves as comfortable as possible. As it left the ground and rose toward the clouds, I cast a parting look at the land and sea below, Hong Kong and the surrounding islands, Kowloon and the New Territories with the mountains of China in the distance. As the landscape receded I reflected on the beauty of land and sea enveloping Hong Kong and, contradistinguished from this, its undiluted commercialism. Then I slipped into a reverie, and I thought of the lovely scenery of Kweilin and Kunming and, set against this, the starkness of the life of the people. Gradually the pictures faded from my mind, and I heard only the roar of the airplane.

About the Author

Born around the time of the foundation of the Republic of China, in the former English colony of British Malaya, Tan Kheng Yeang was educated in an English school. His father was from China but had immigrated to Malaya and had become a successful businessman, involved in various activities, including as a rubber merchant. From his early days the author was interested in literature and philosophy. As his interest evolved to science, he decided to study civil engineering at the University of Hong Kong, as he felt he needed a practical career.

After the Japanese occupied Hong Kong, he went into Free China where he found work in an office constructing roads and later an airfield in Guangxi Province. After the war ended in 1945, he returned to Malaya and became an engineer in the City Council of Georgetown, Penang. After his retirement, he worked as an engineering consultant. He is the author of twelve books that reflect the broad range of his interests and talent.